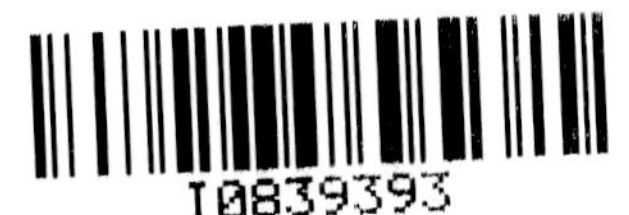

I'M JUST CHILLIN'
CAPYBARAS COLORING BOOK

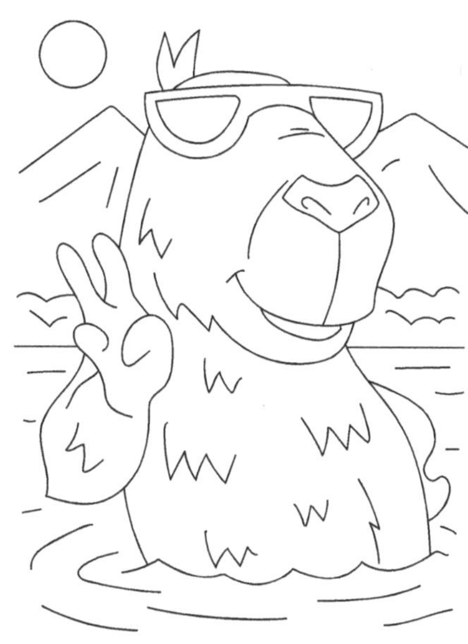

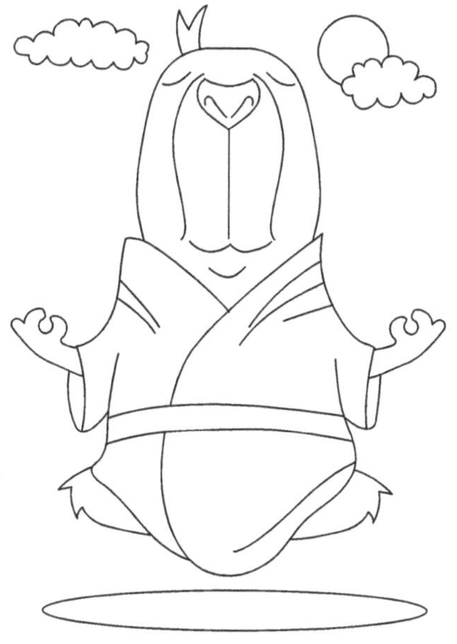

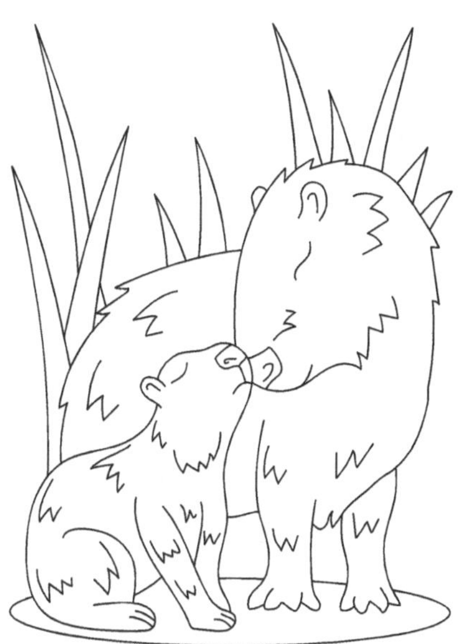

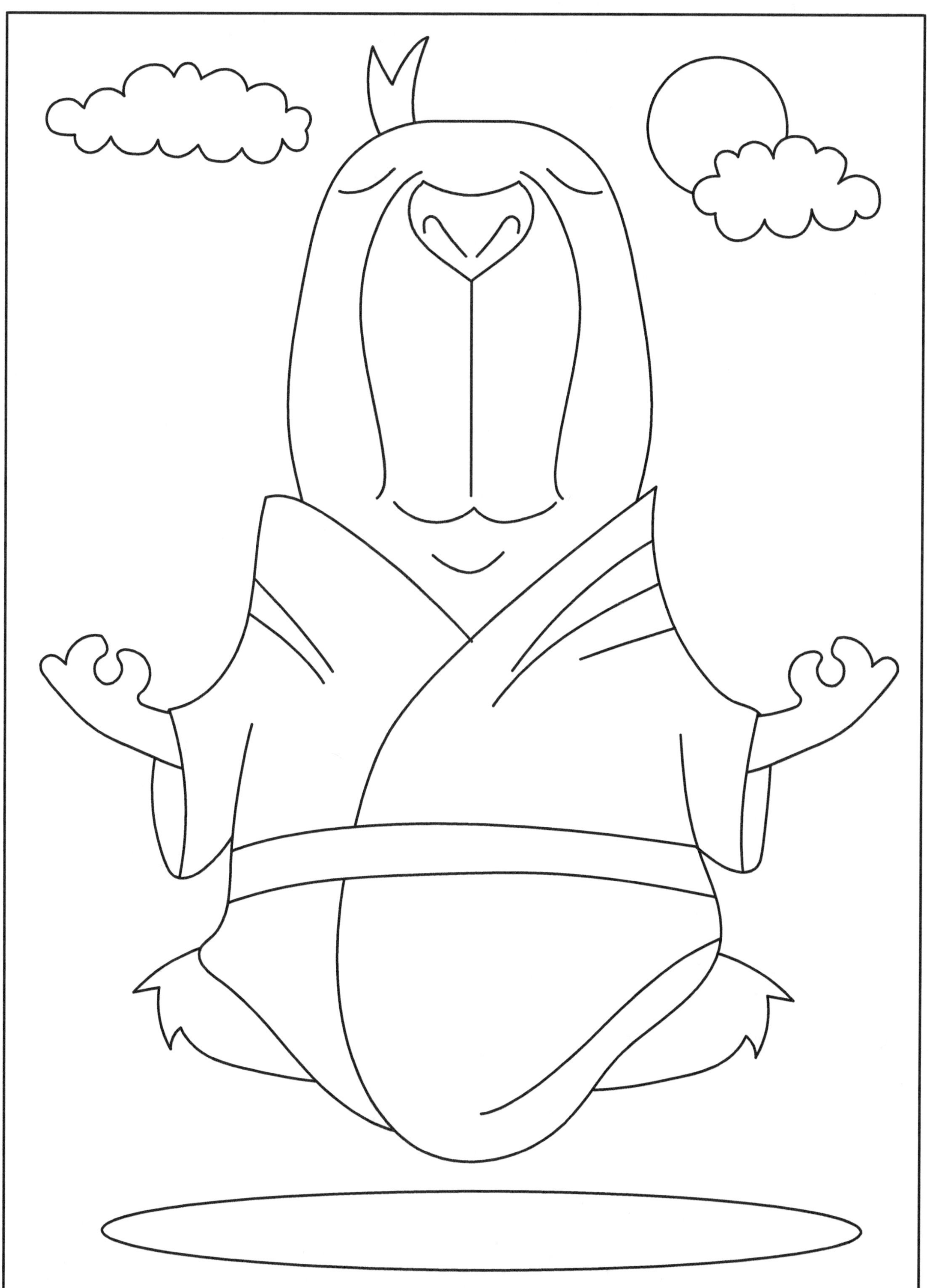

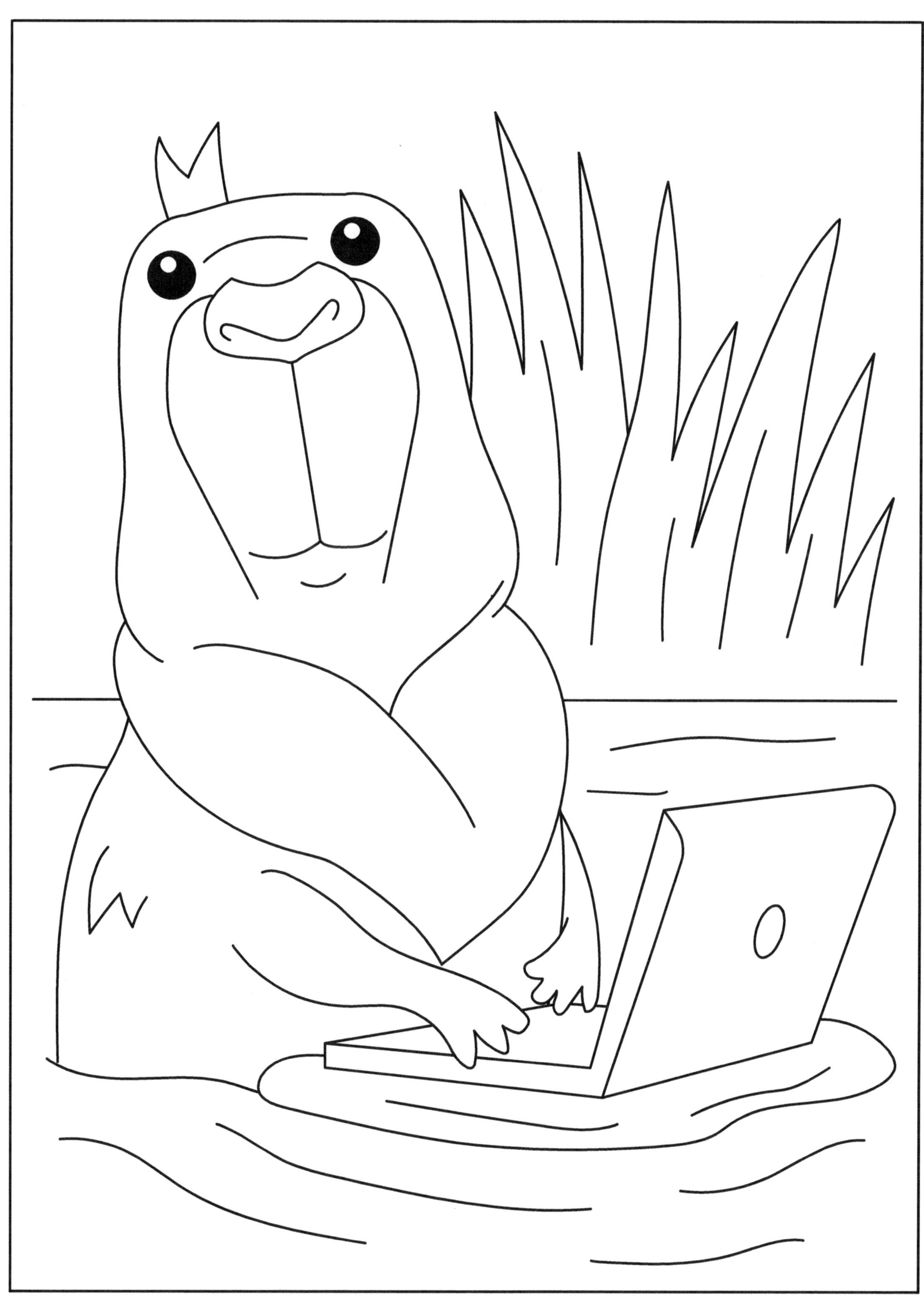

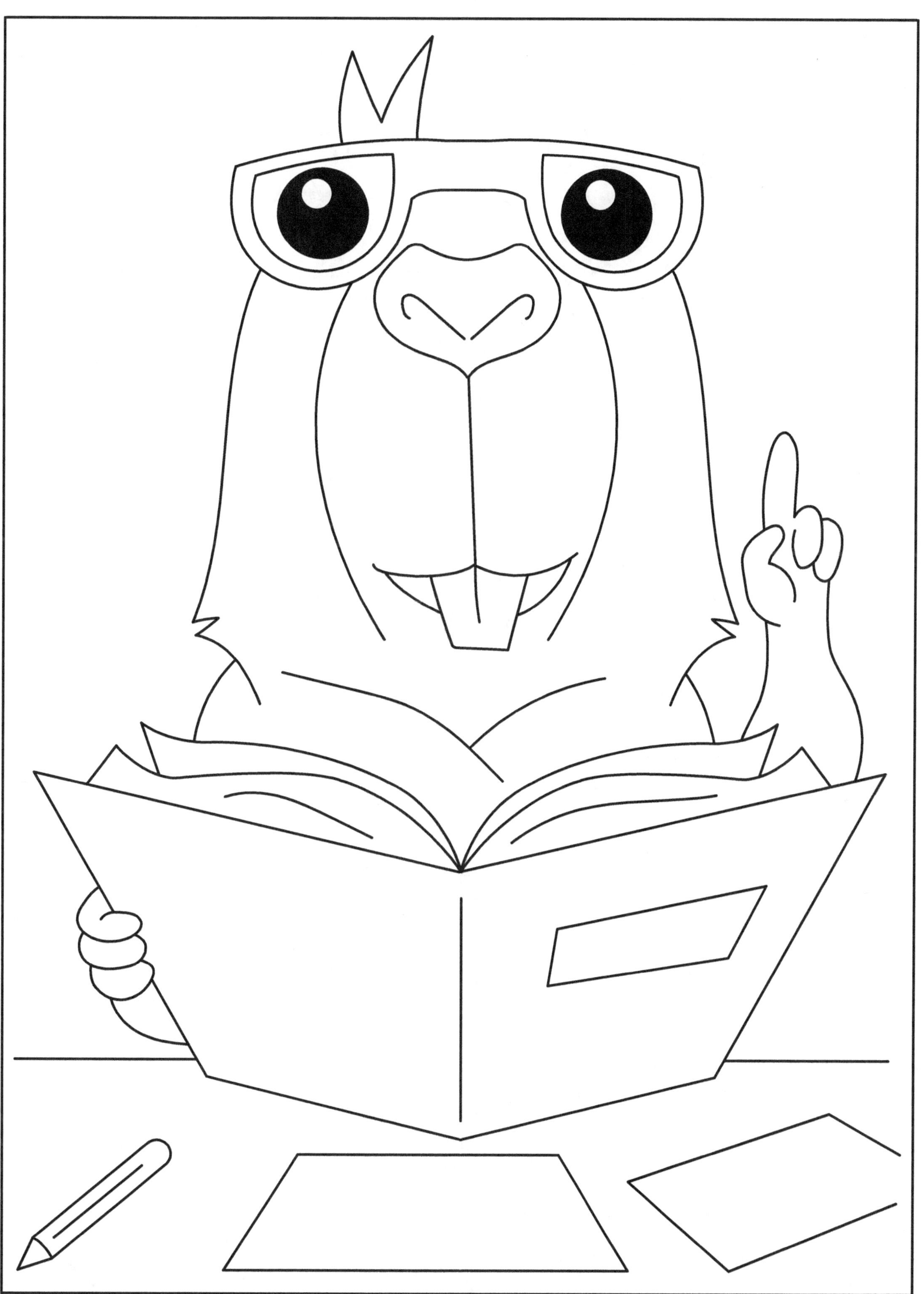

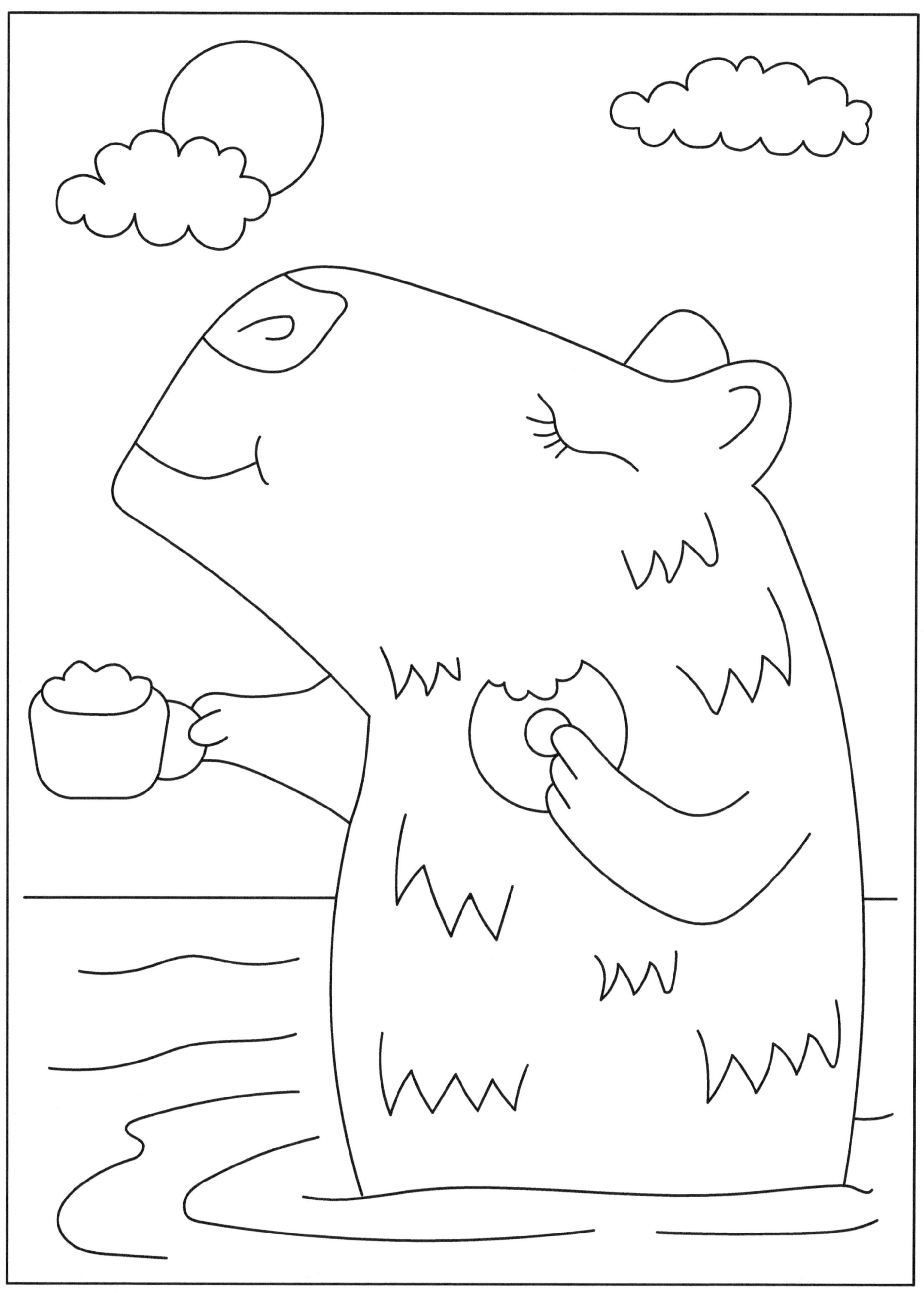

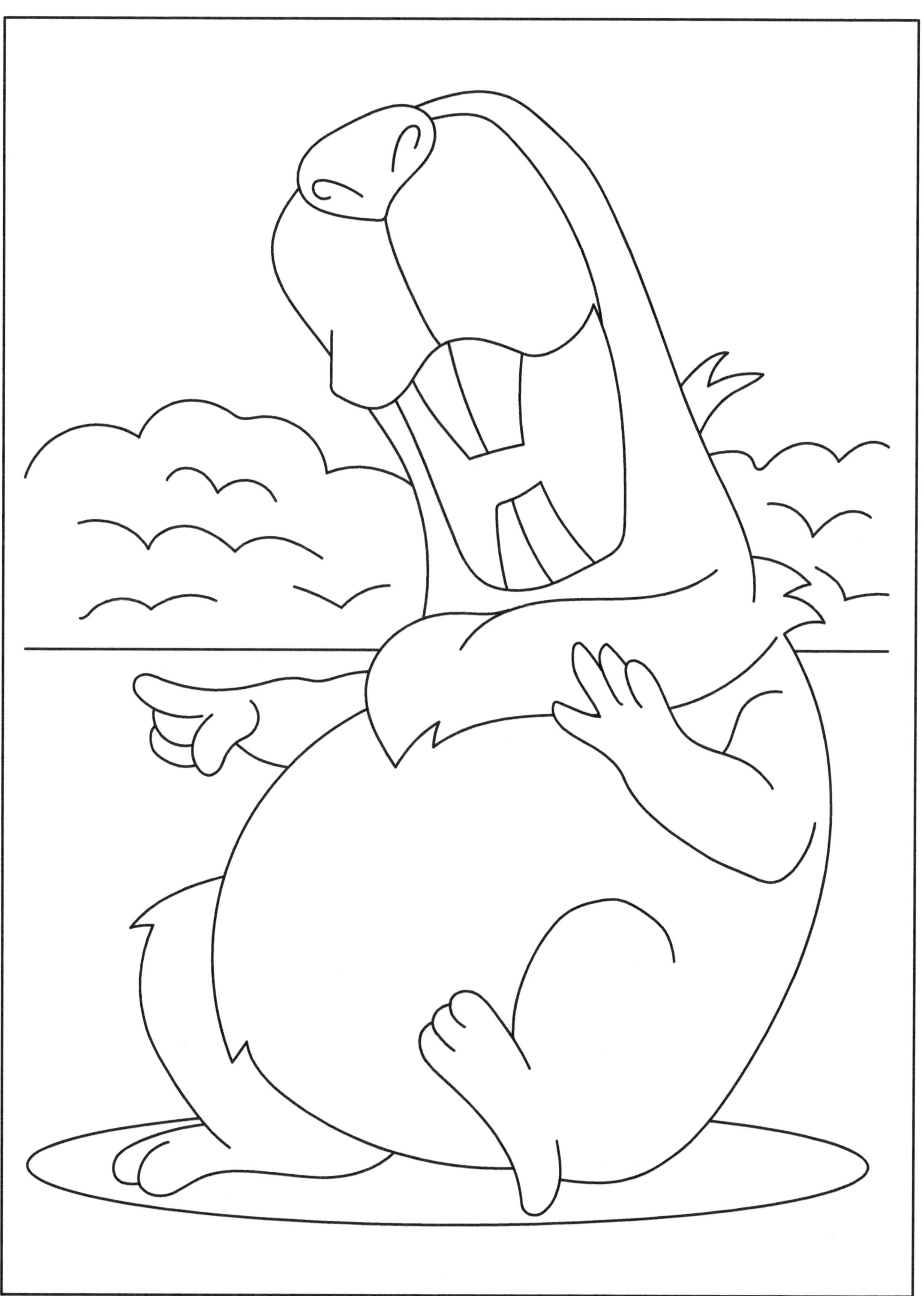

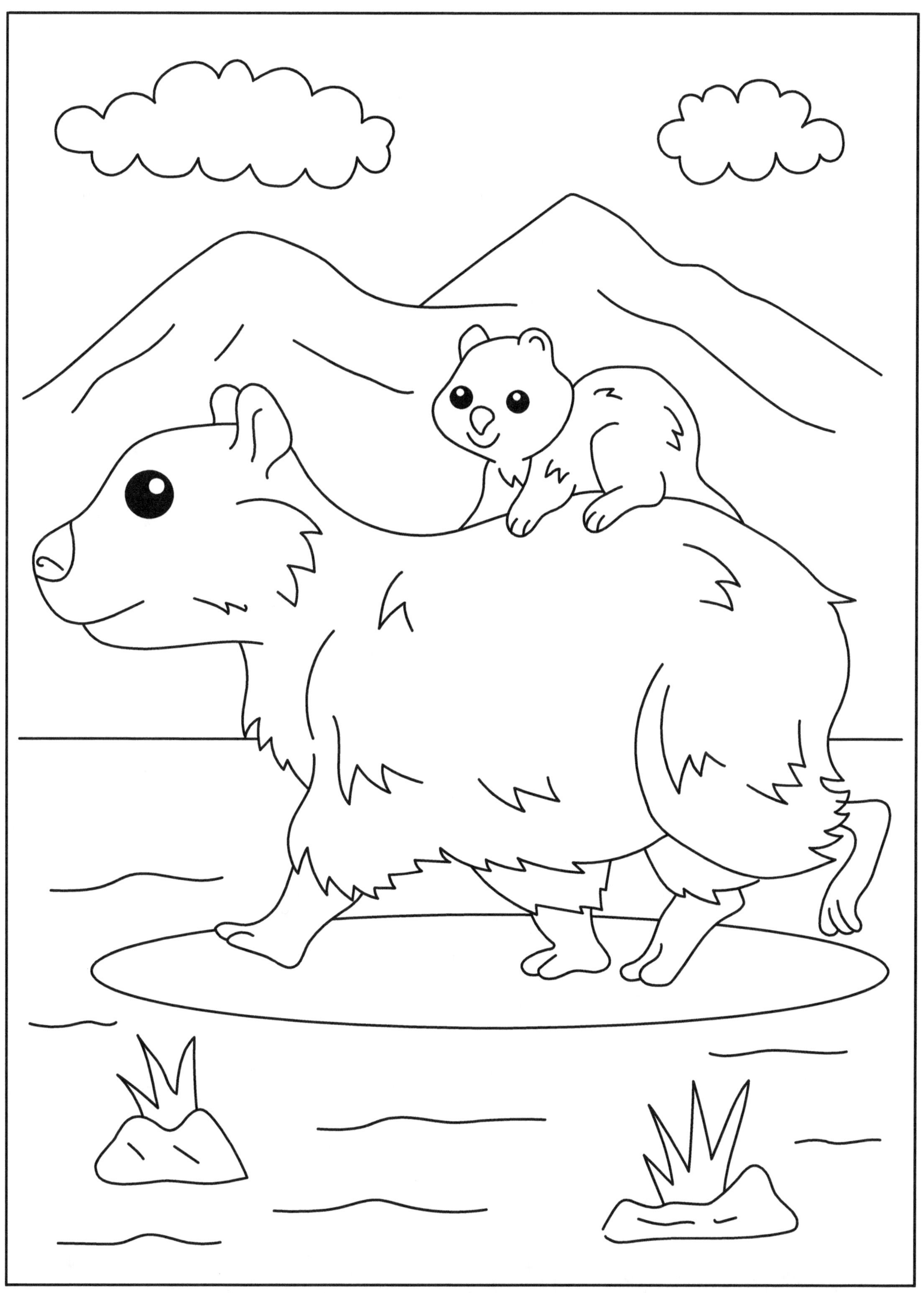

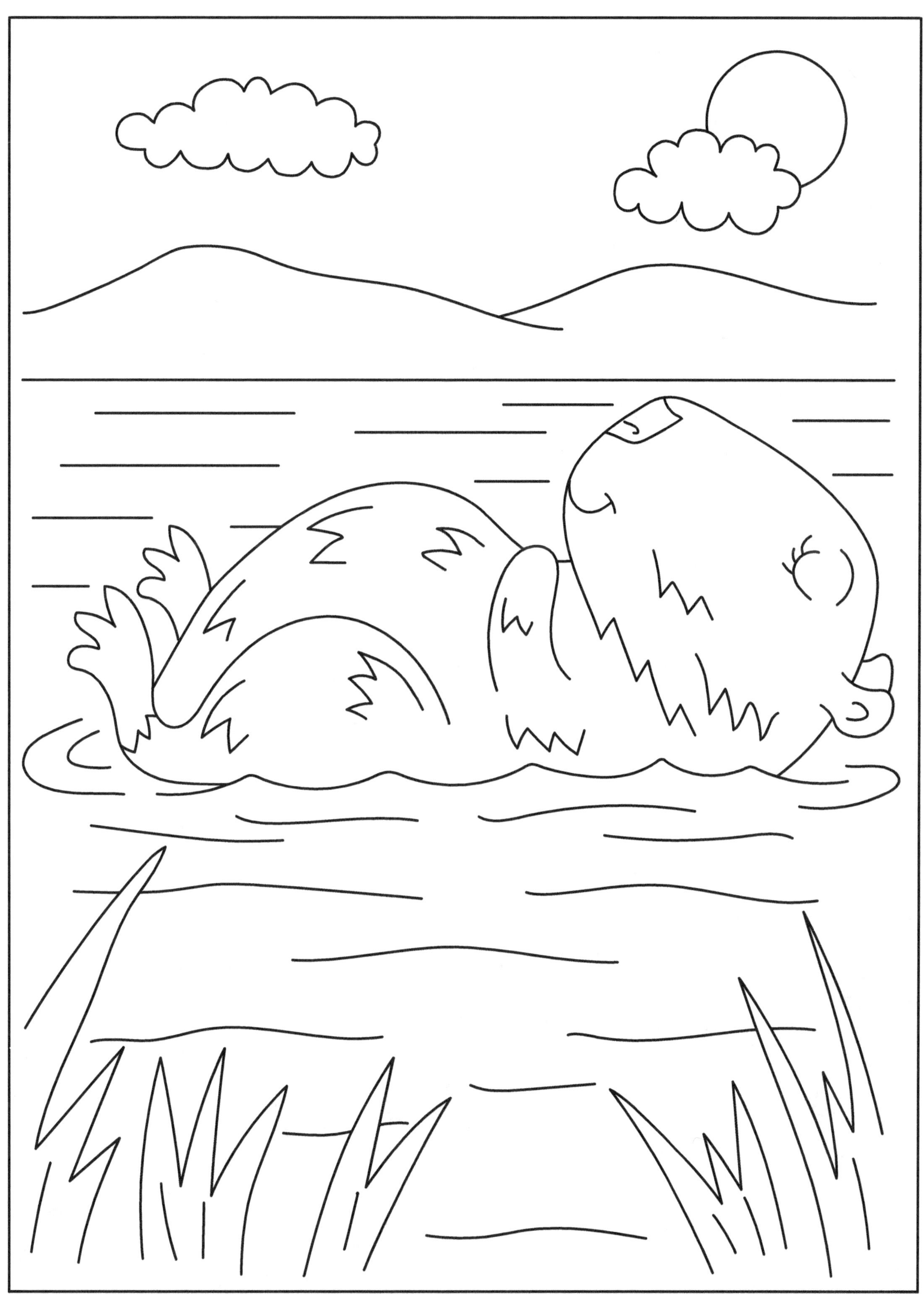

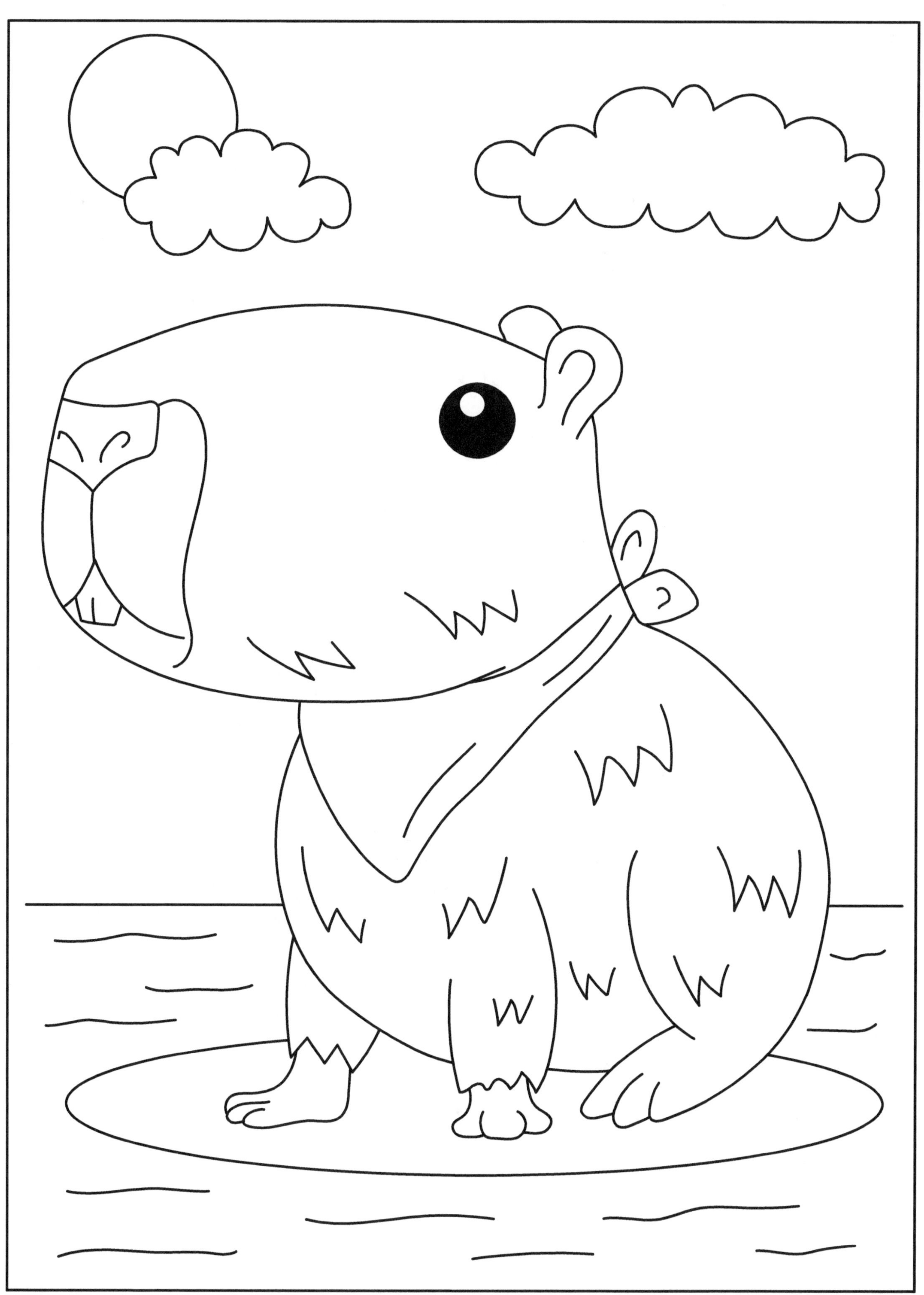

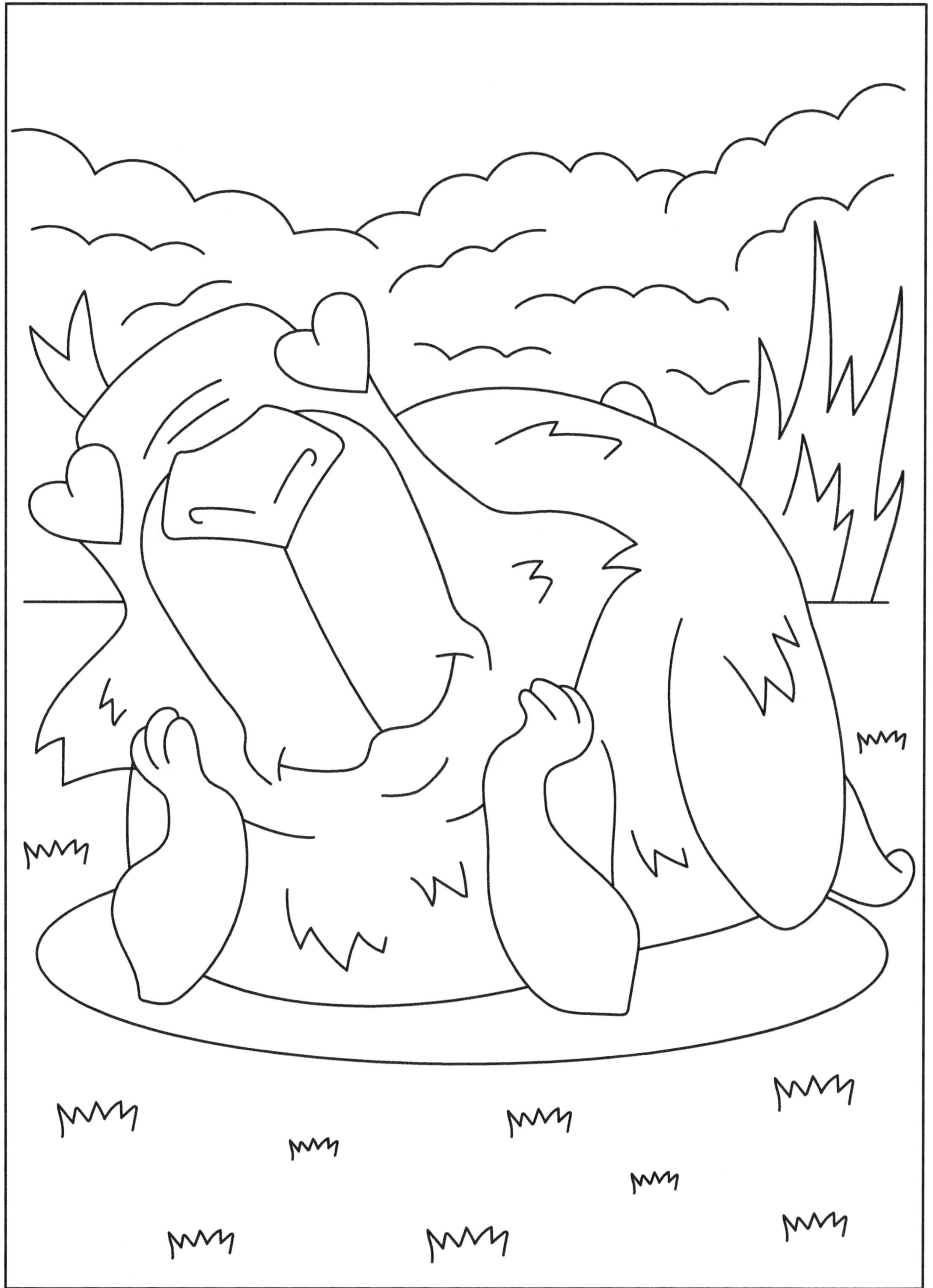

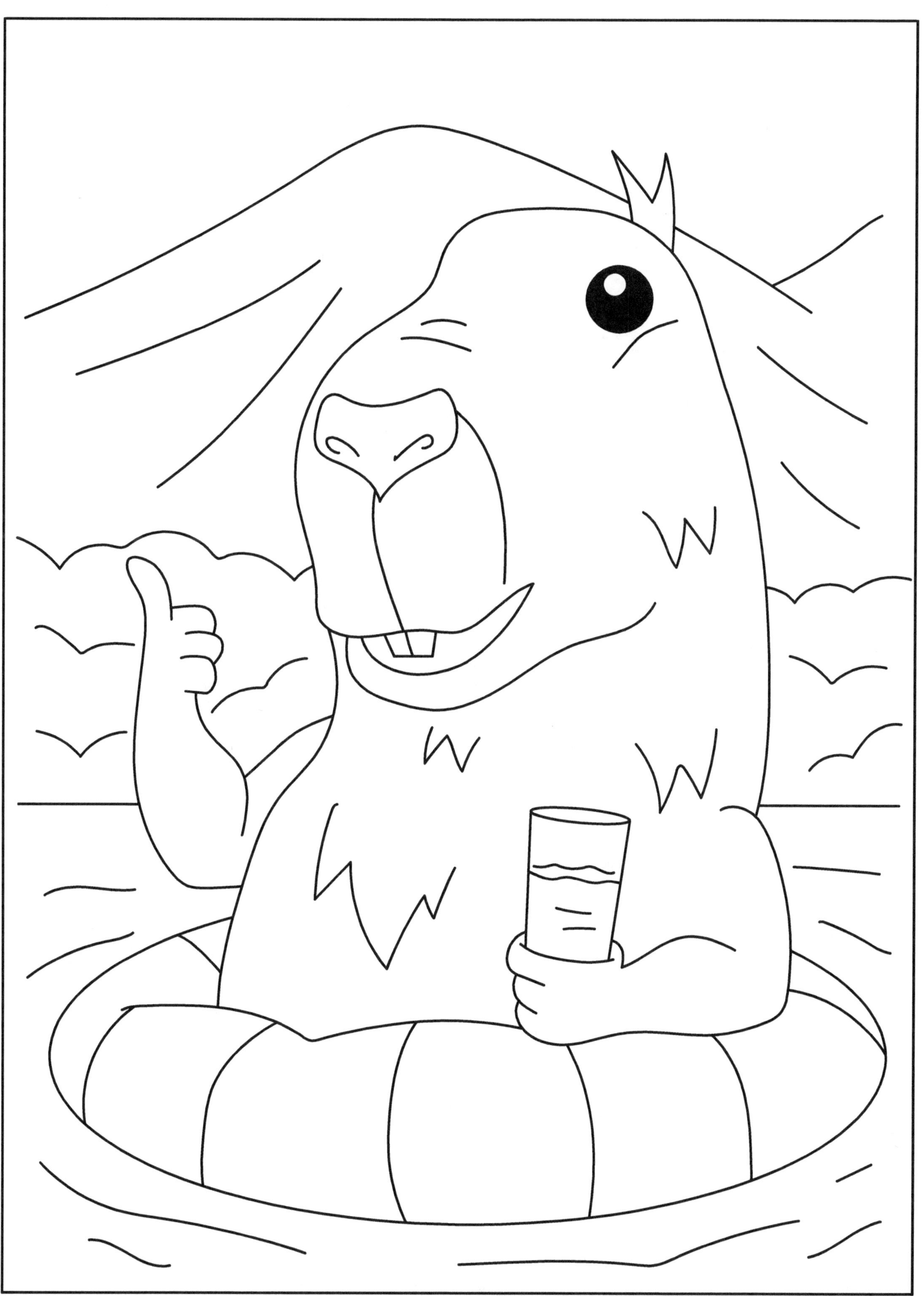

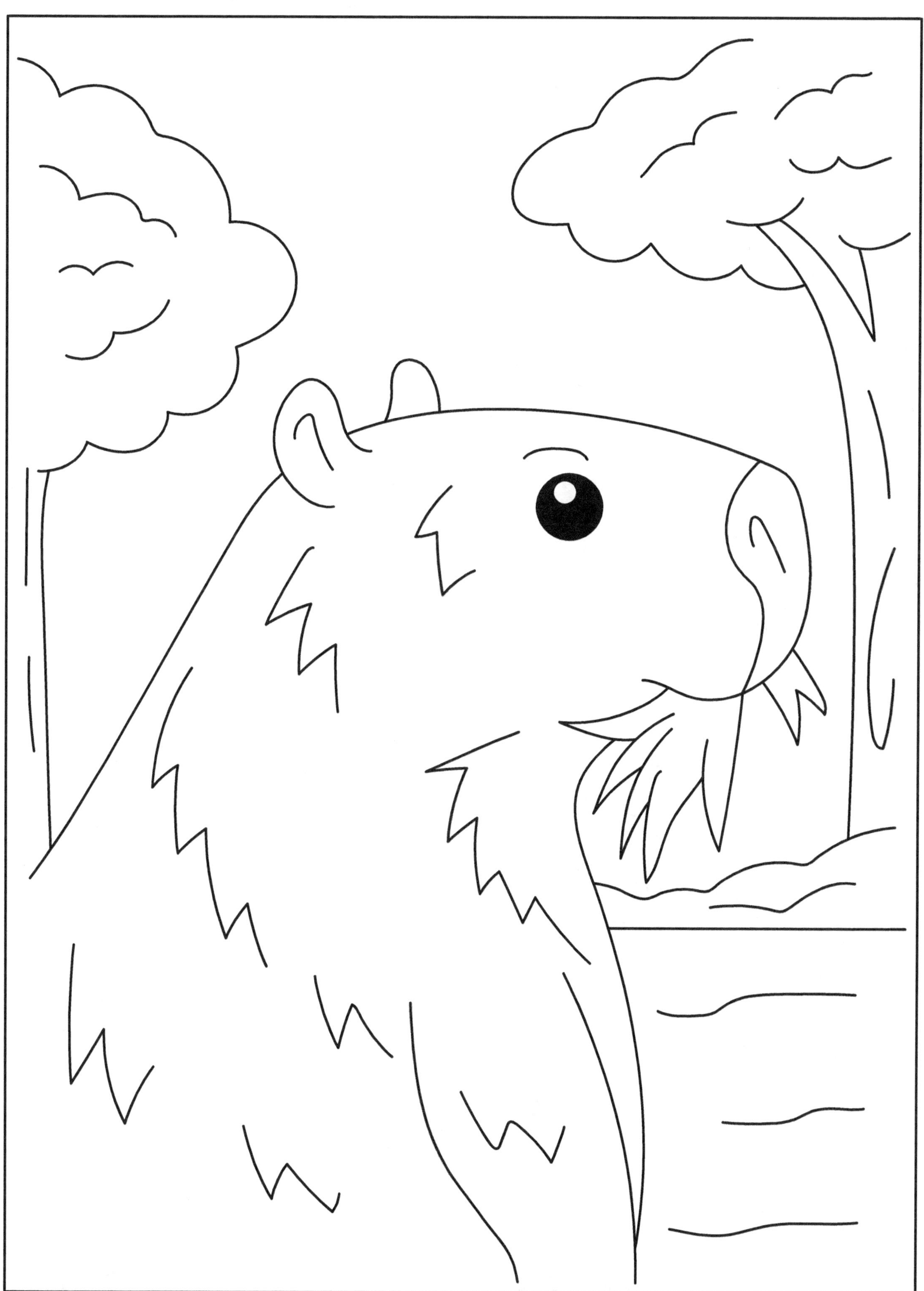

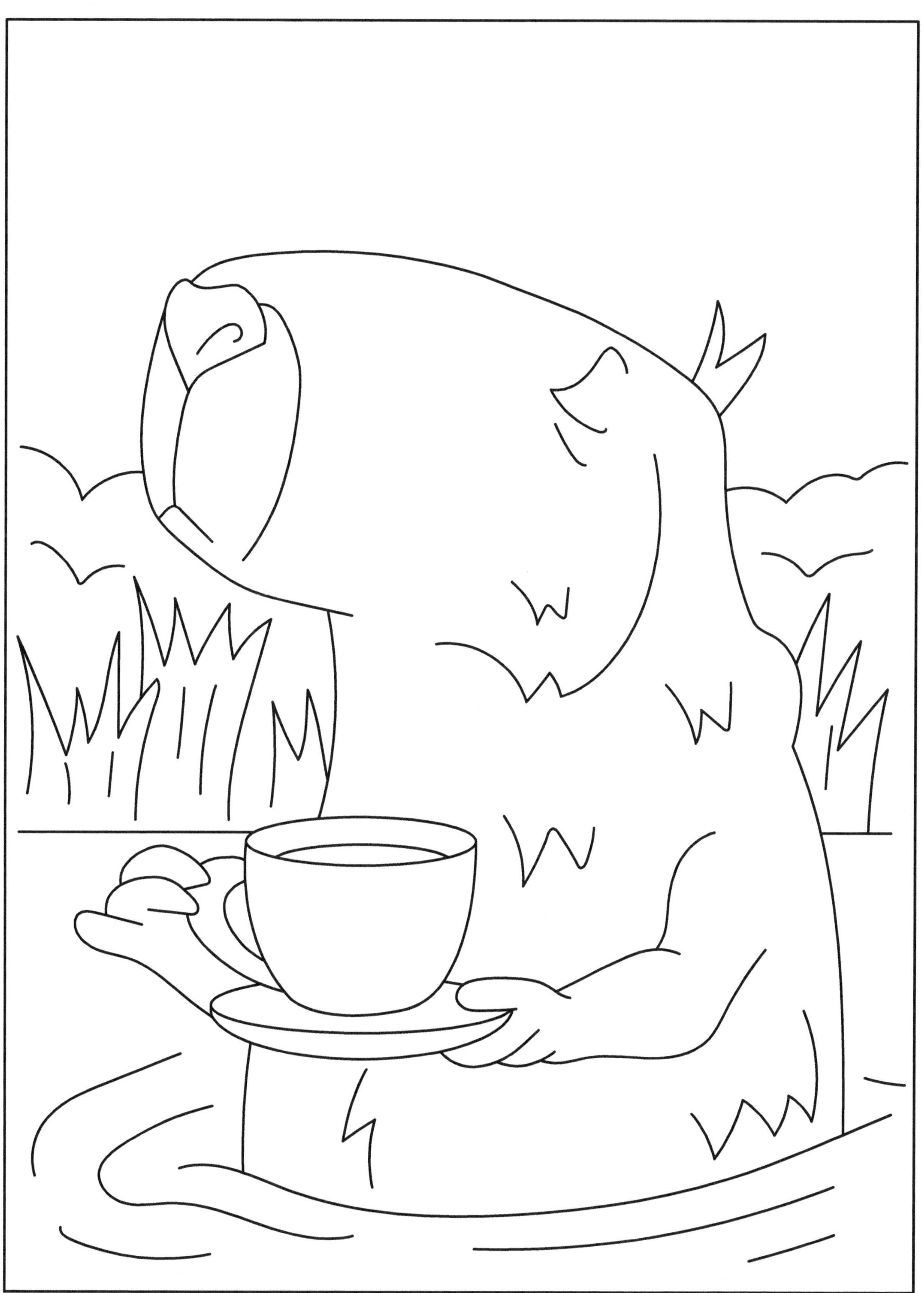

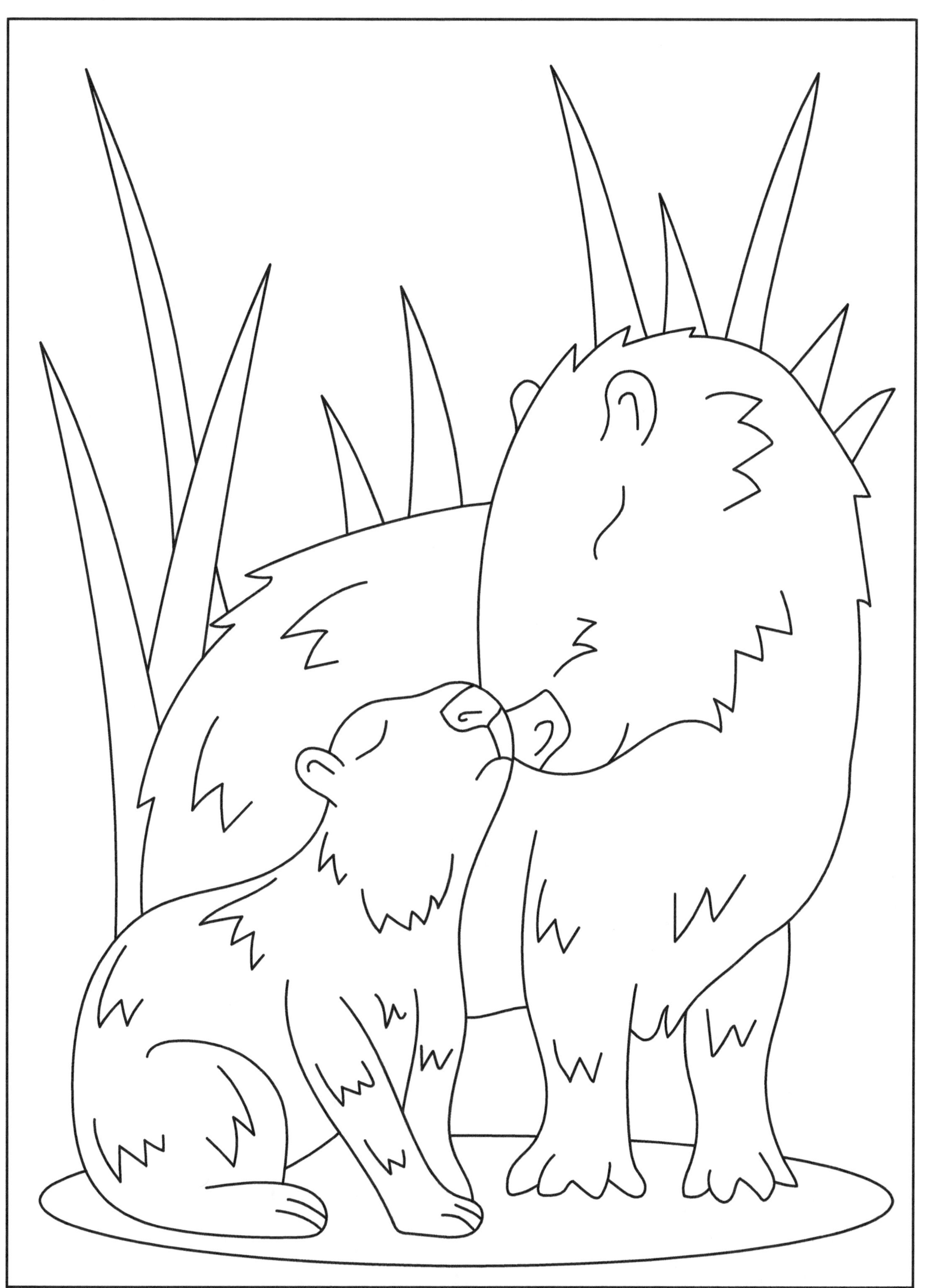

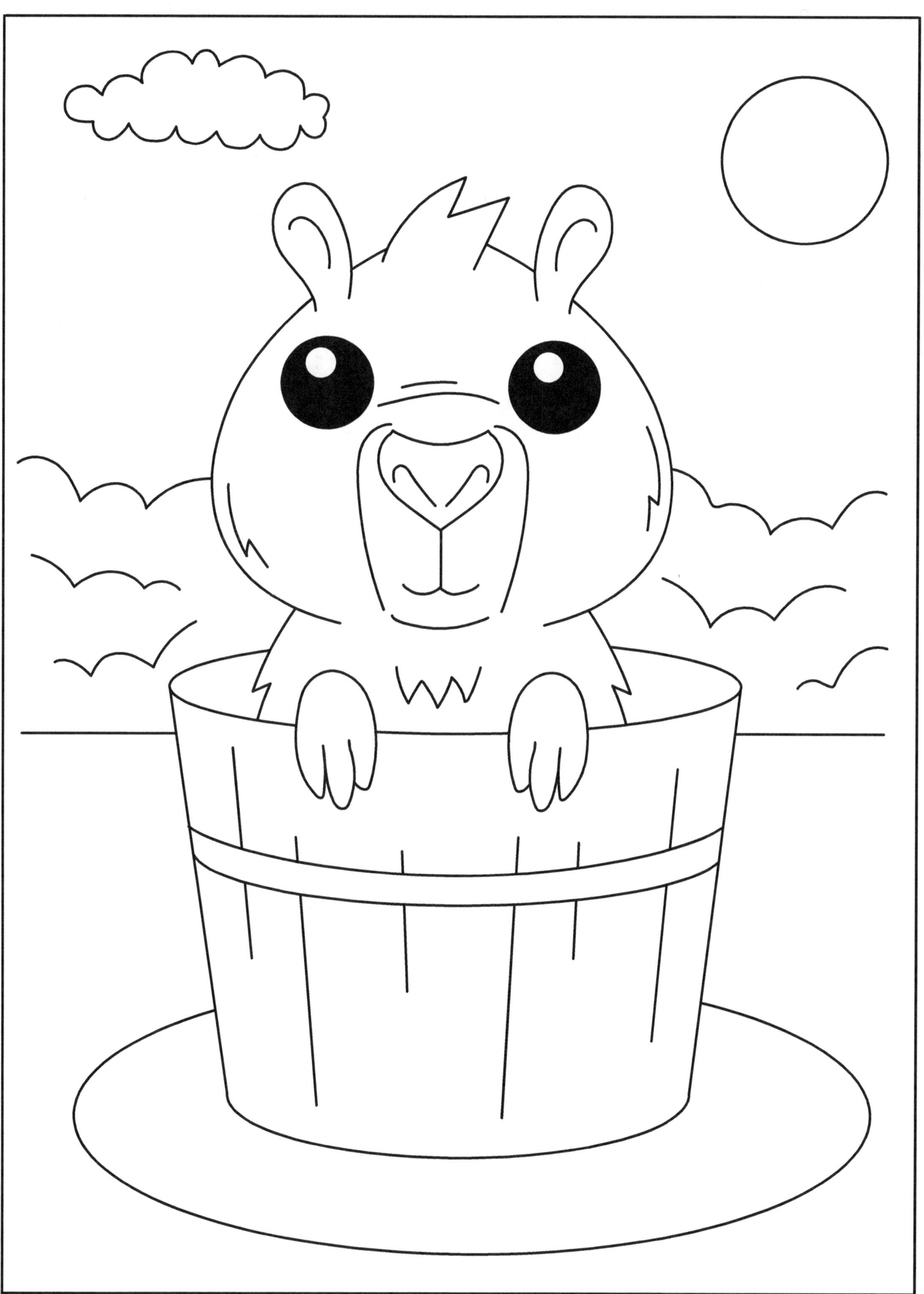

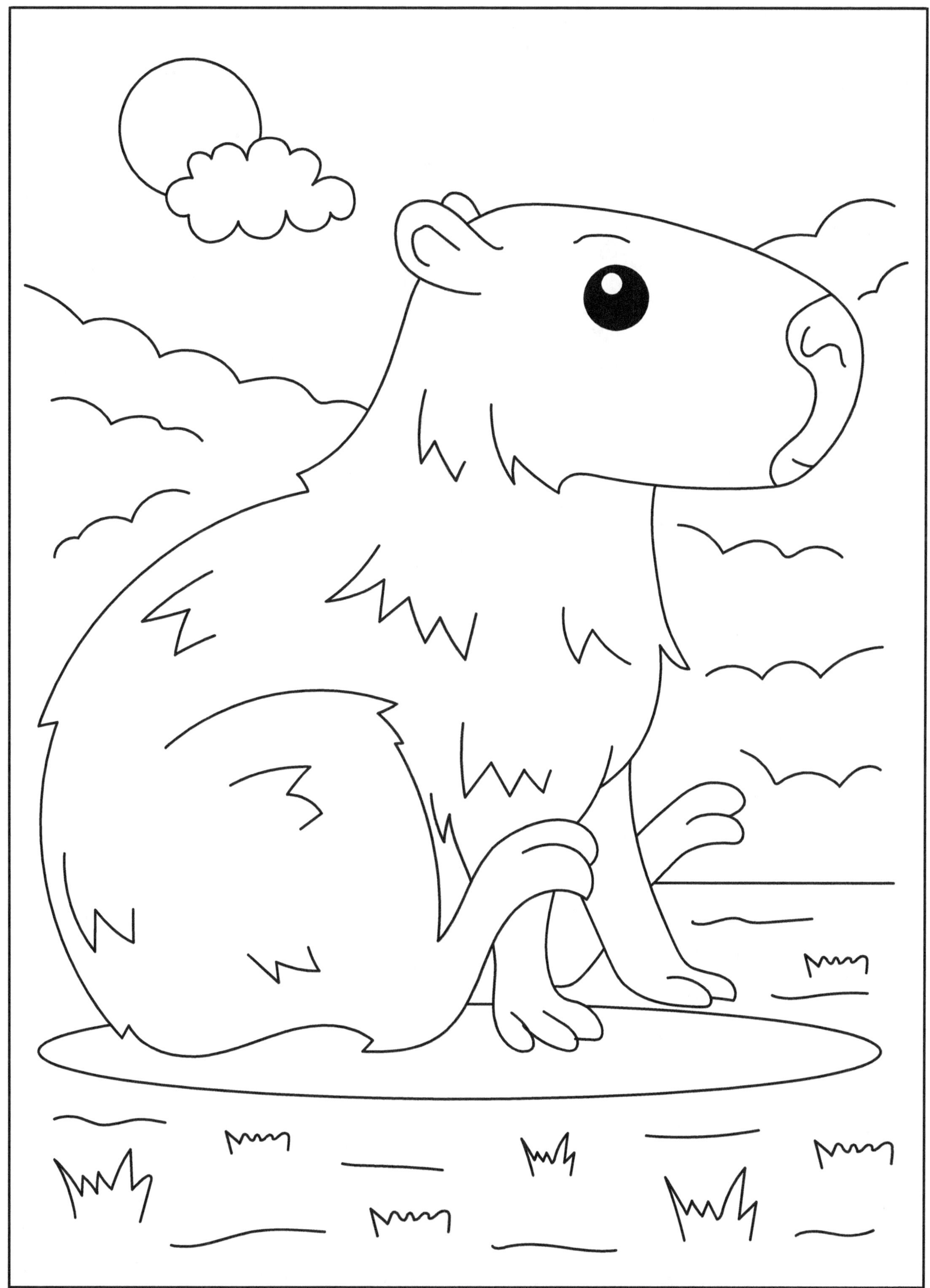

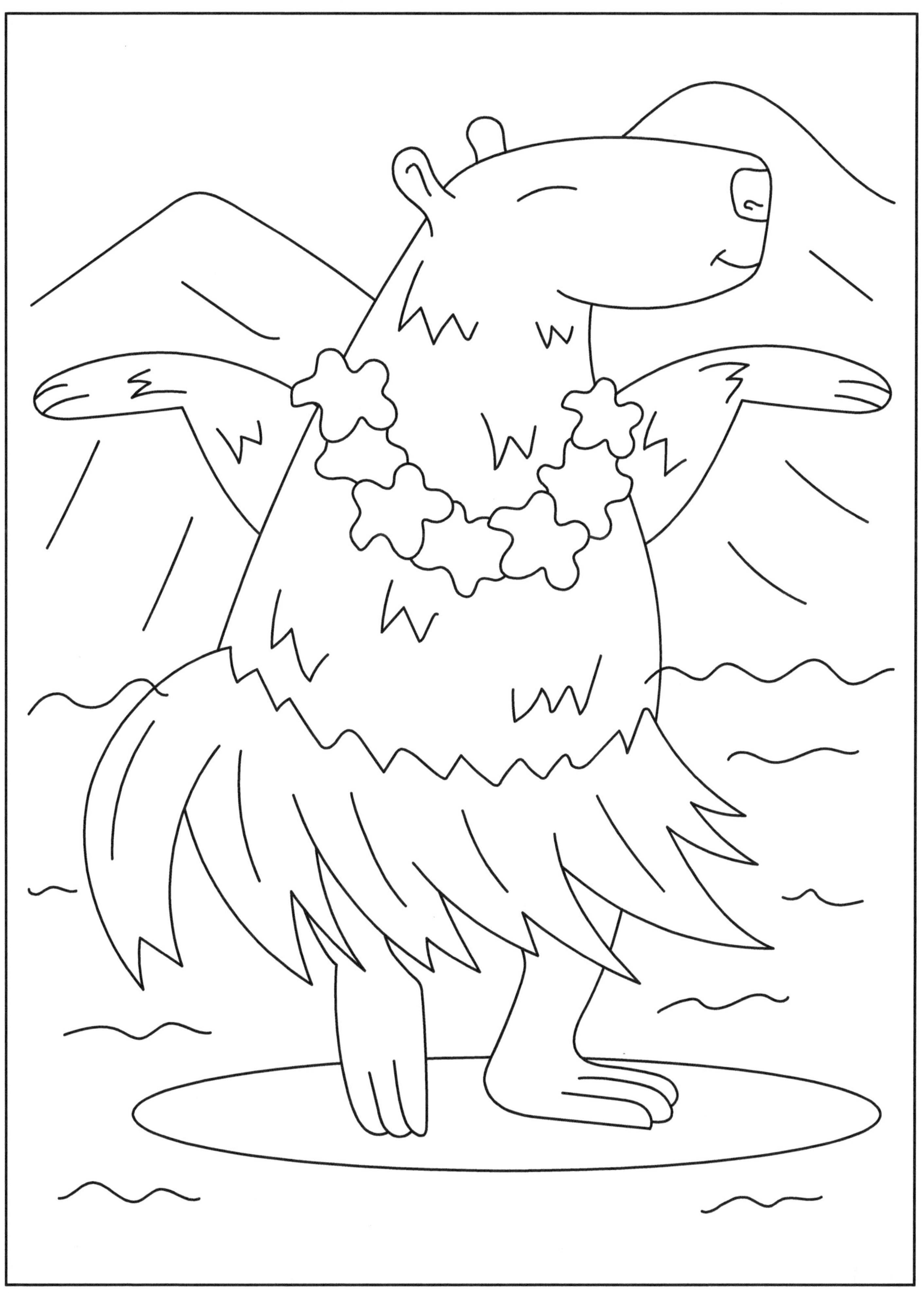

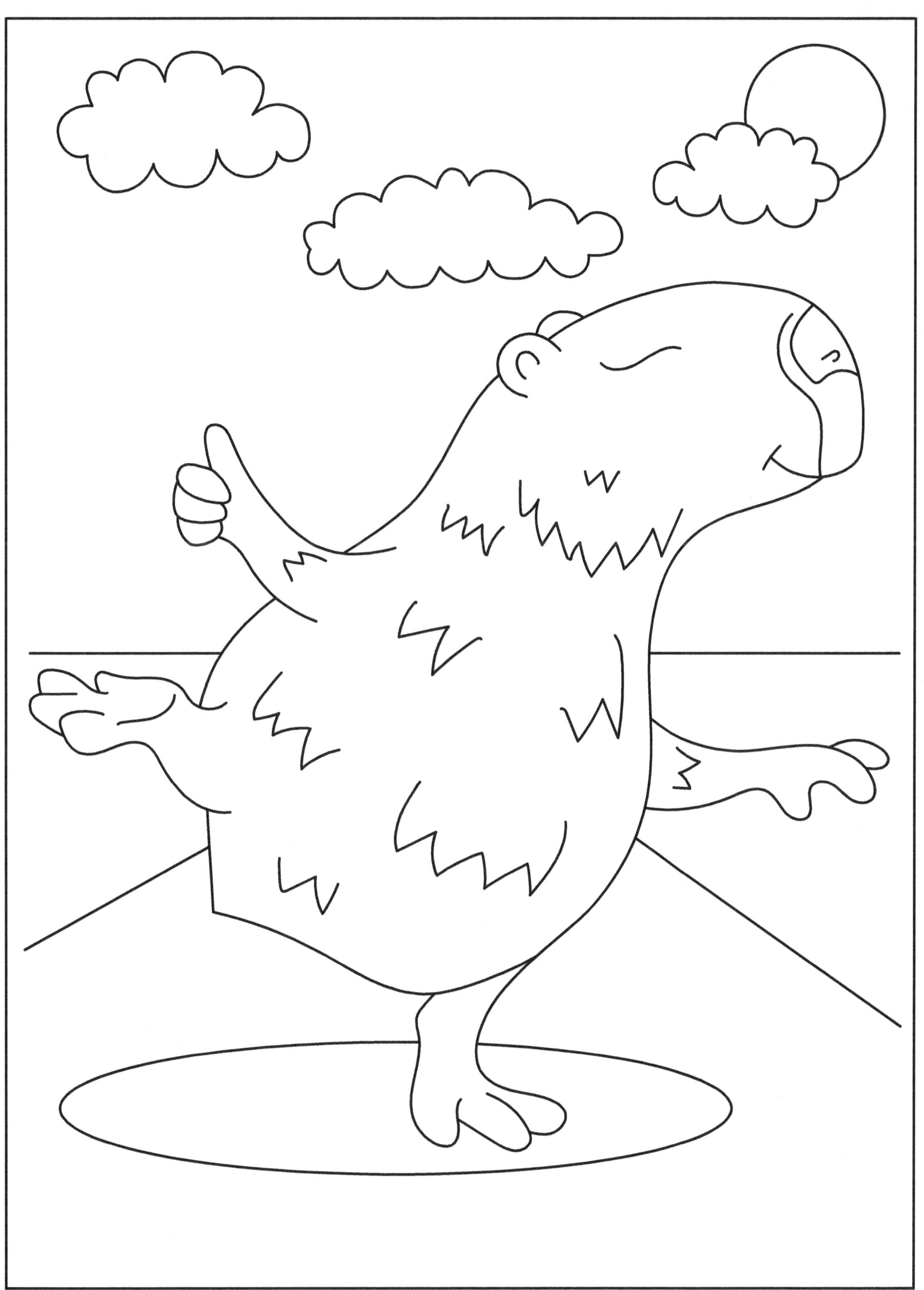

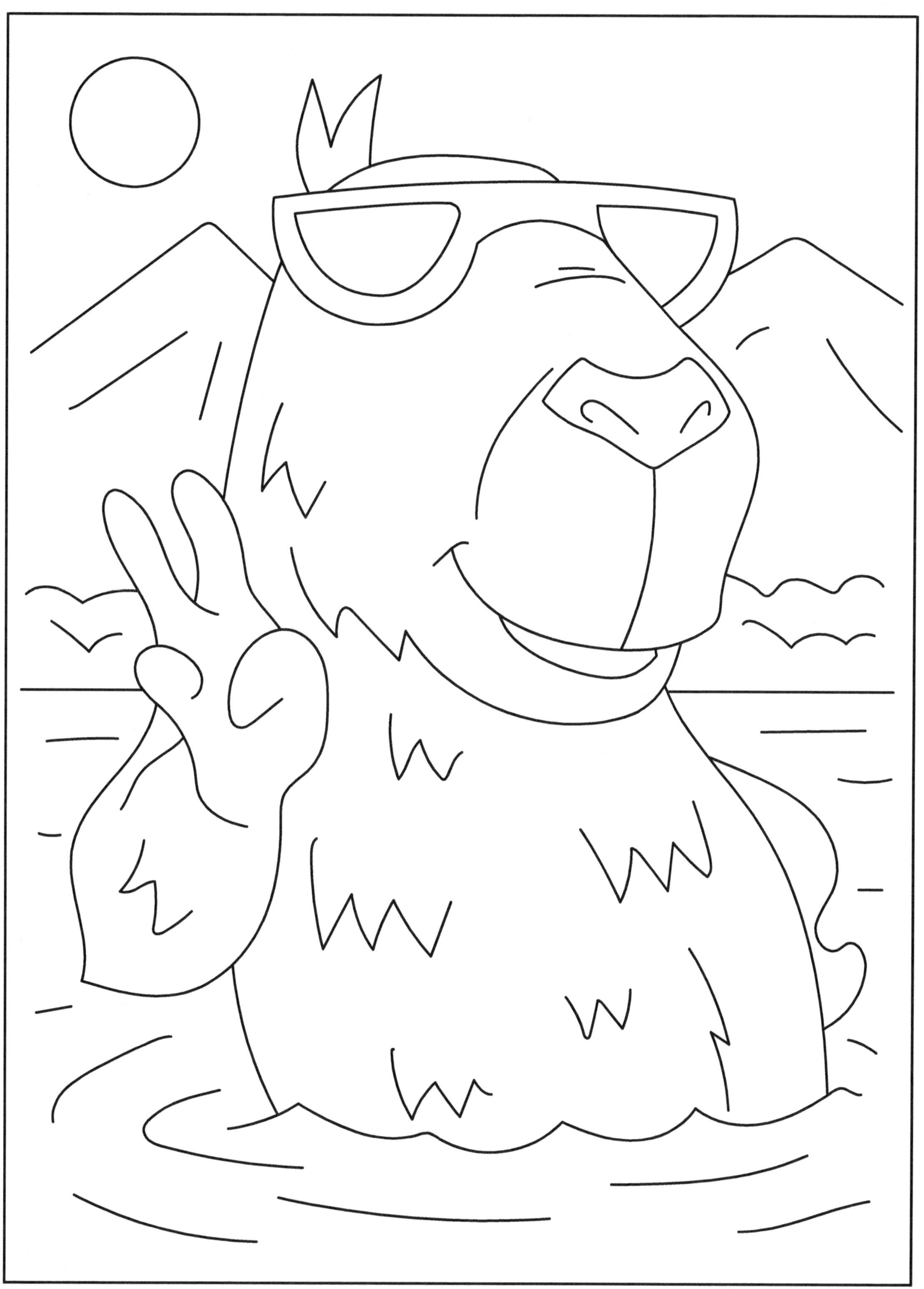

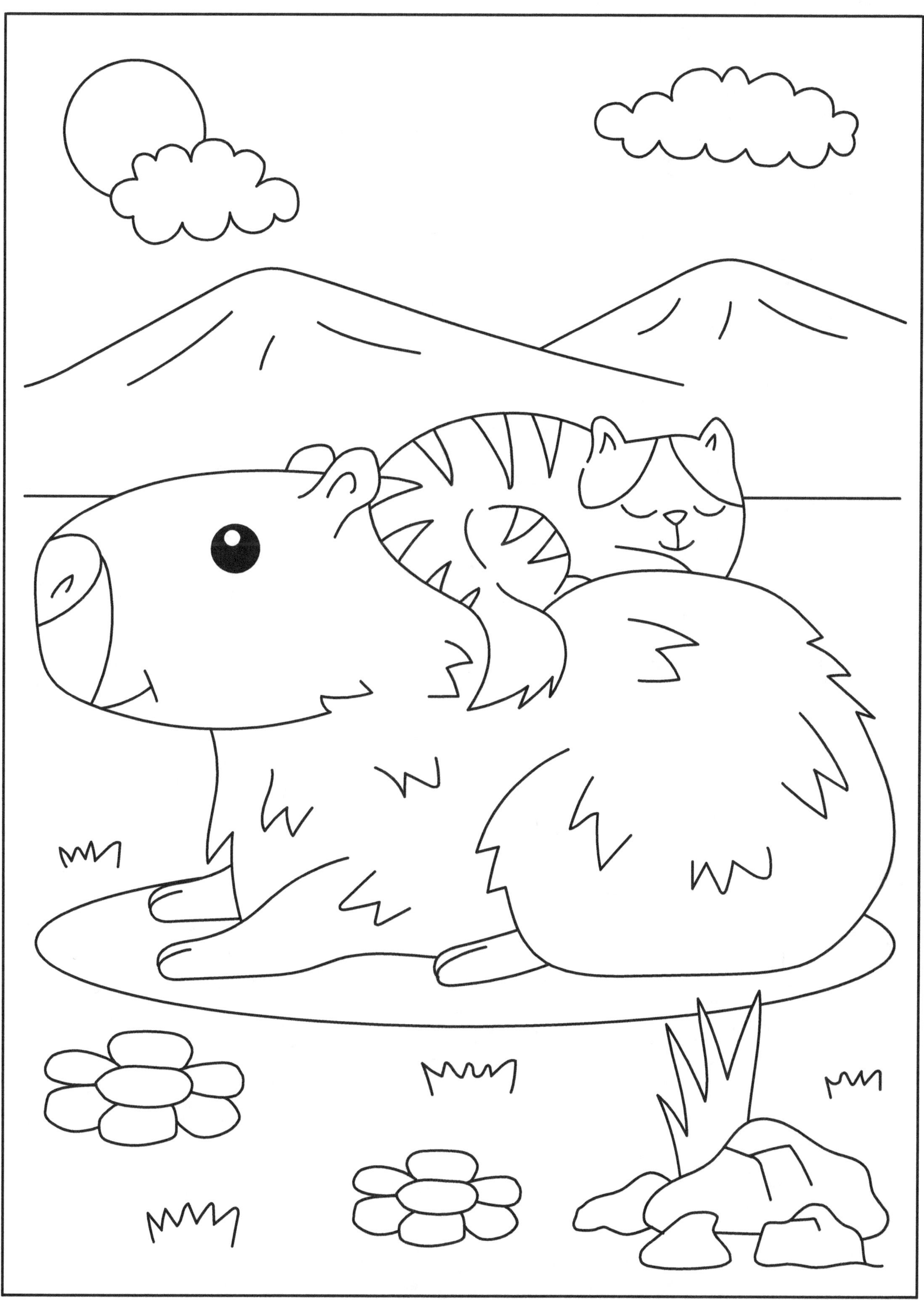

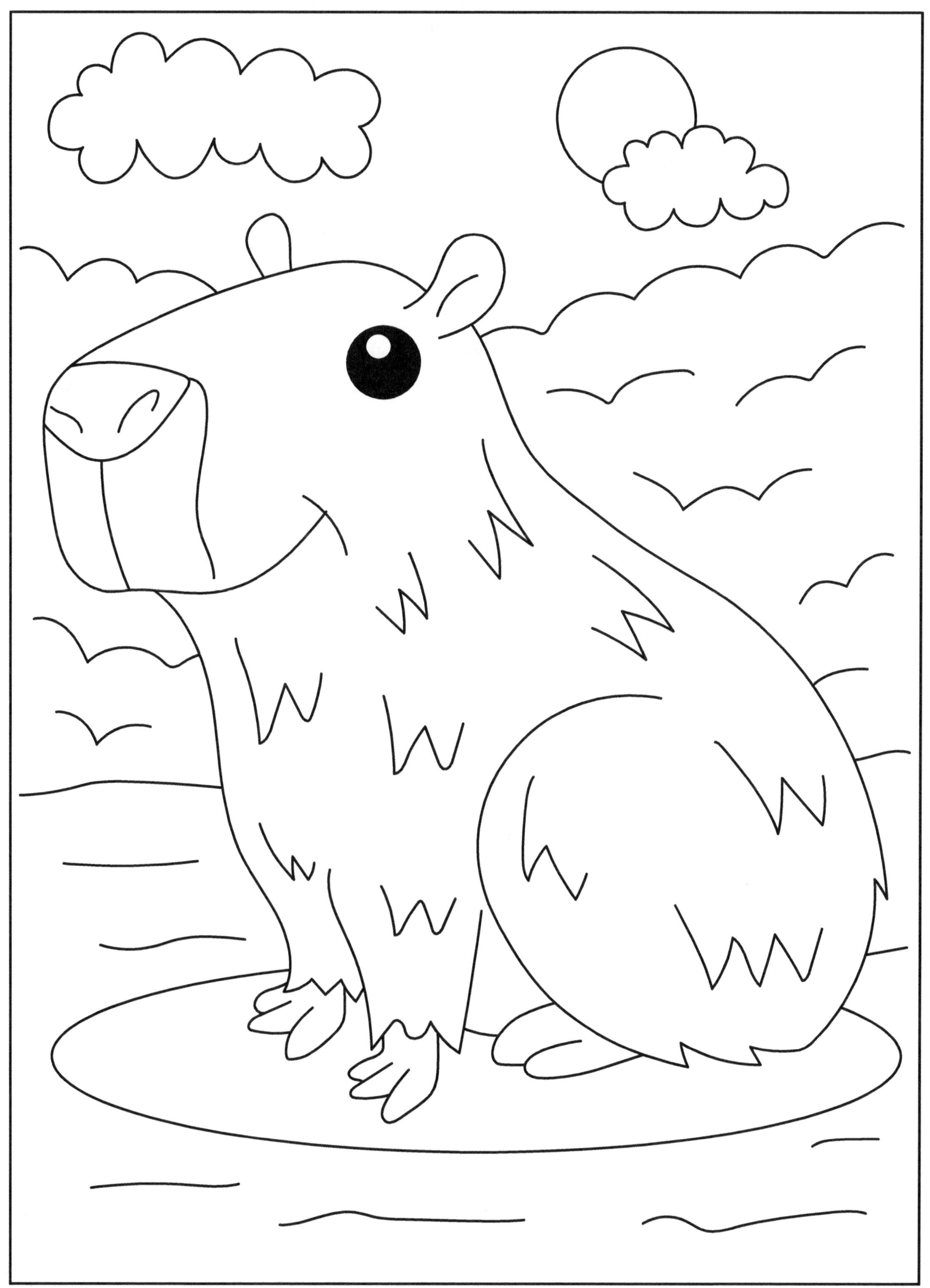

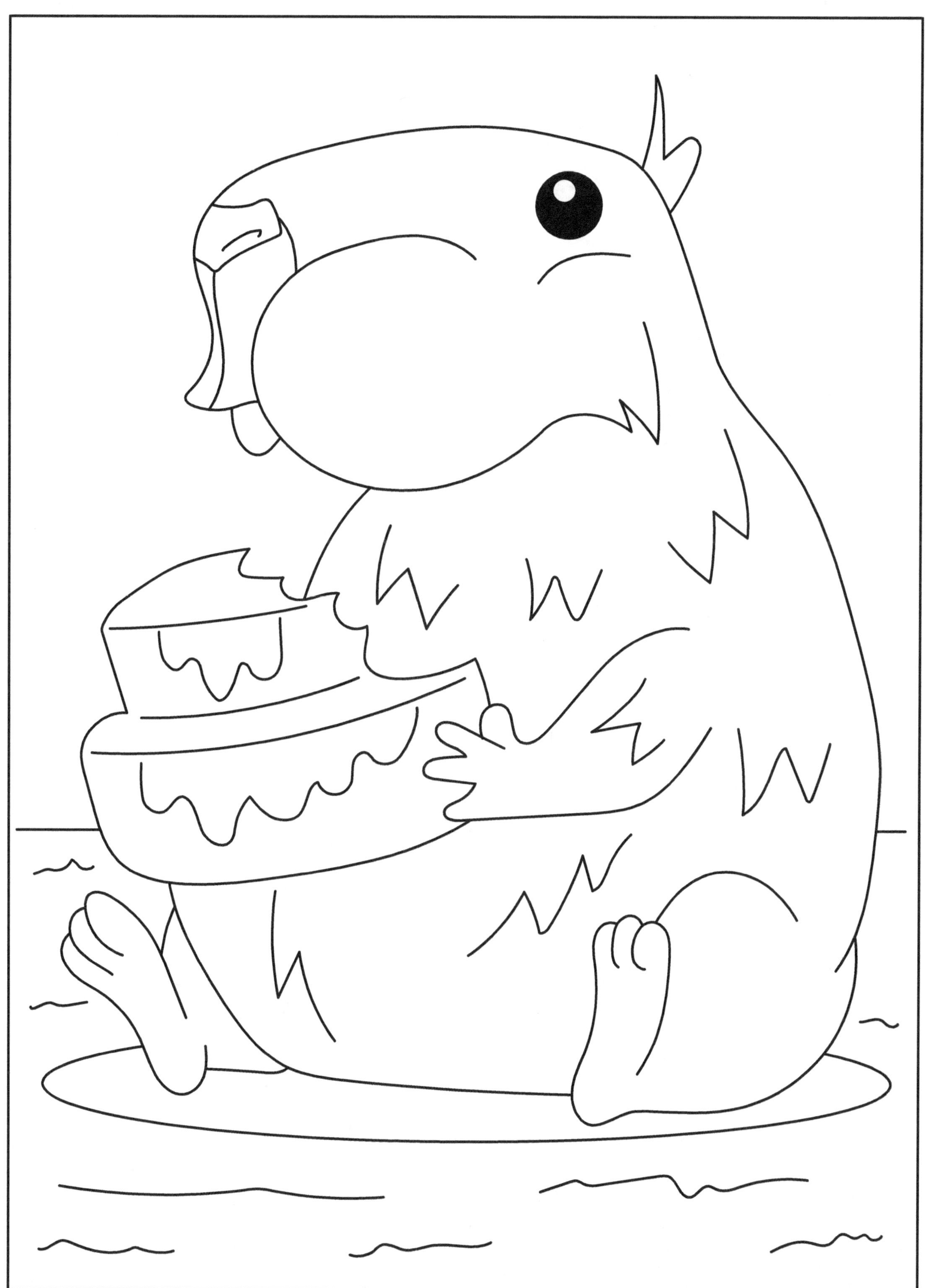

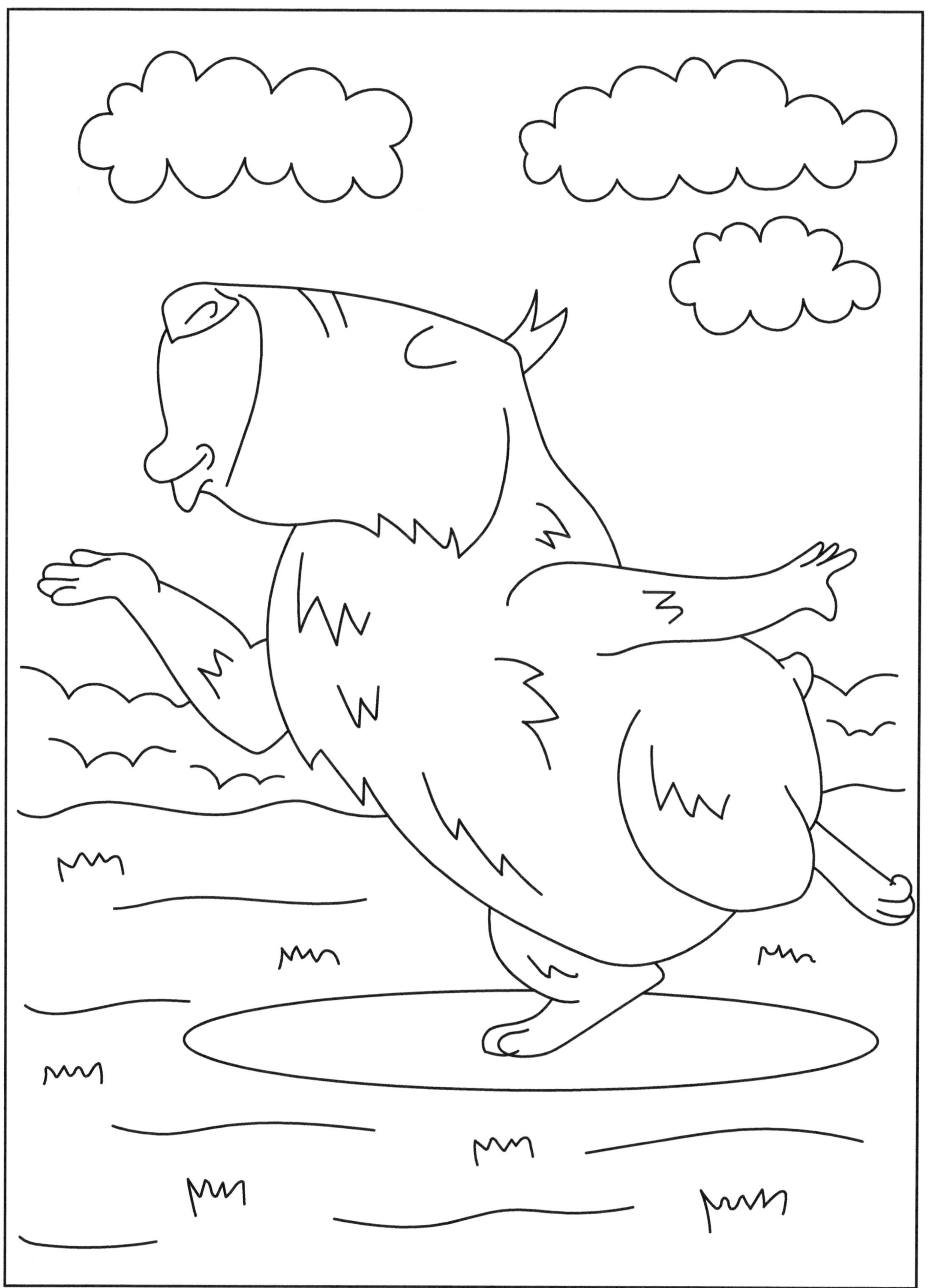

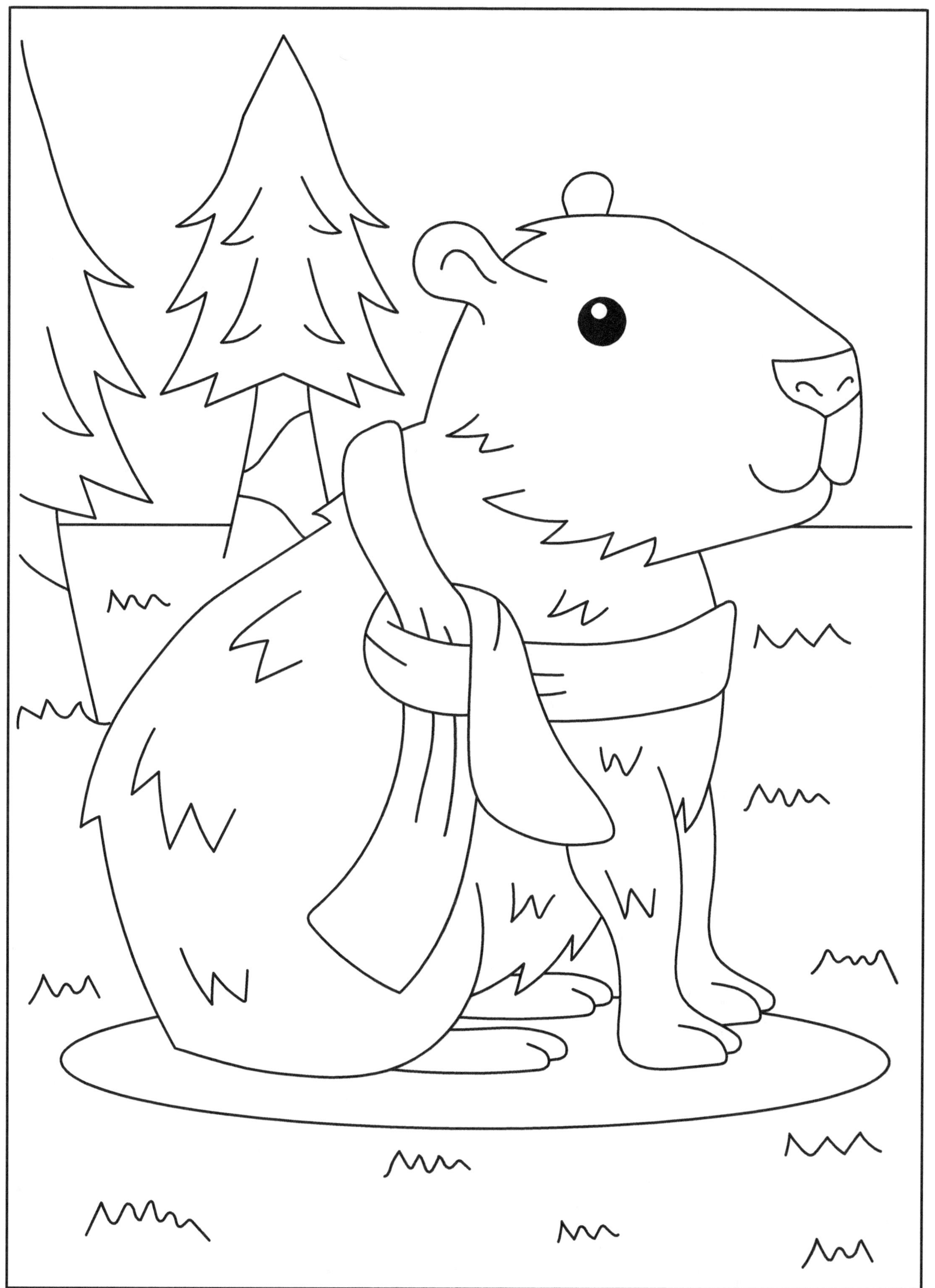

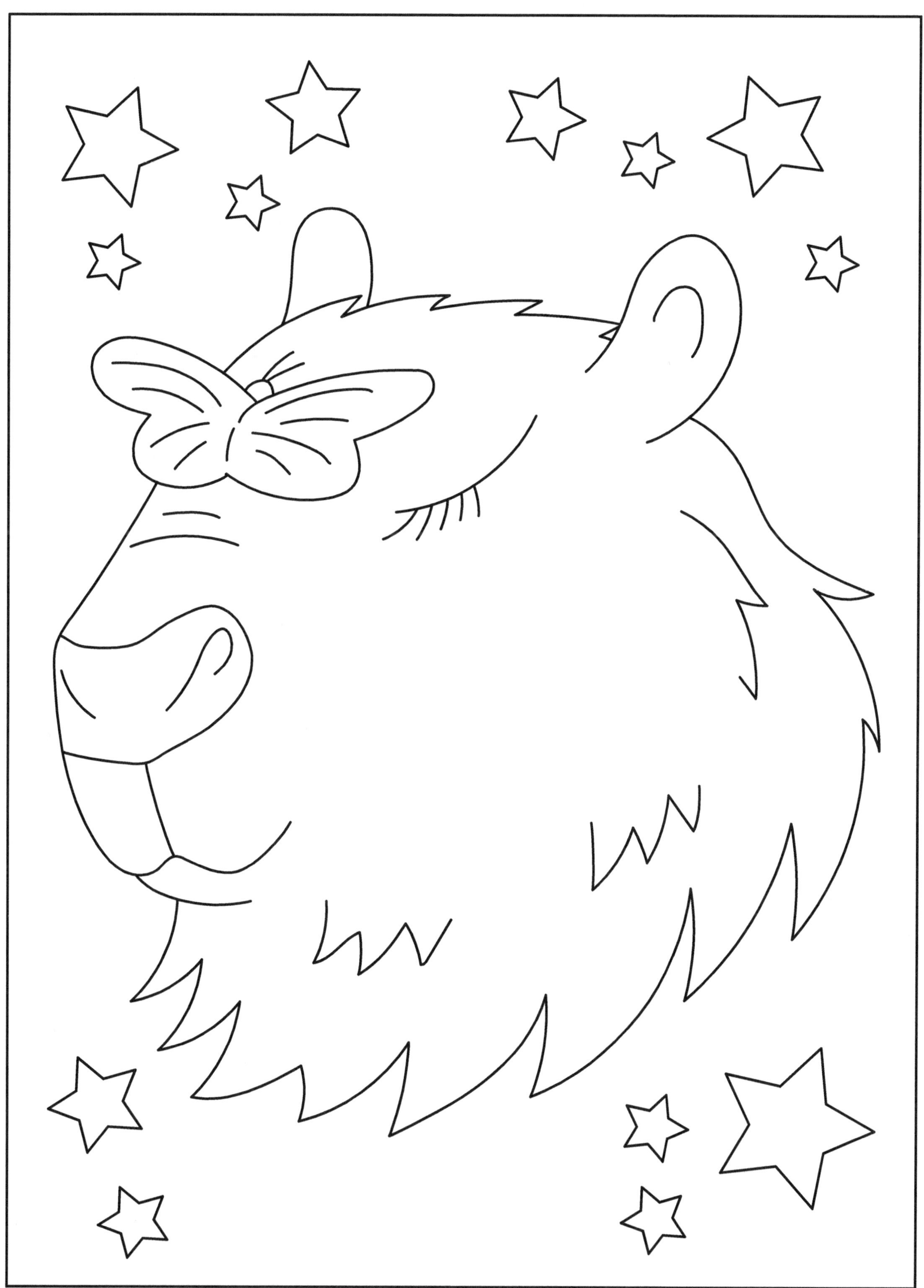

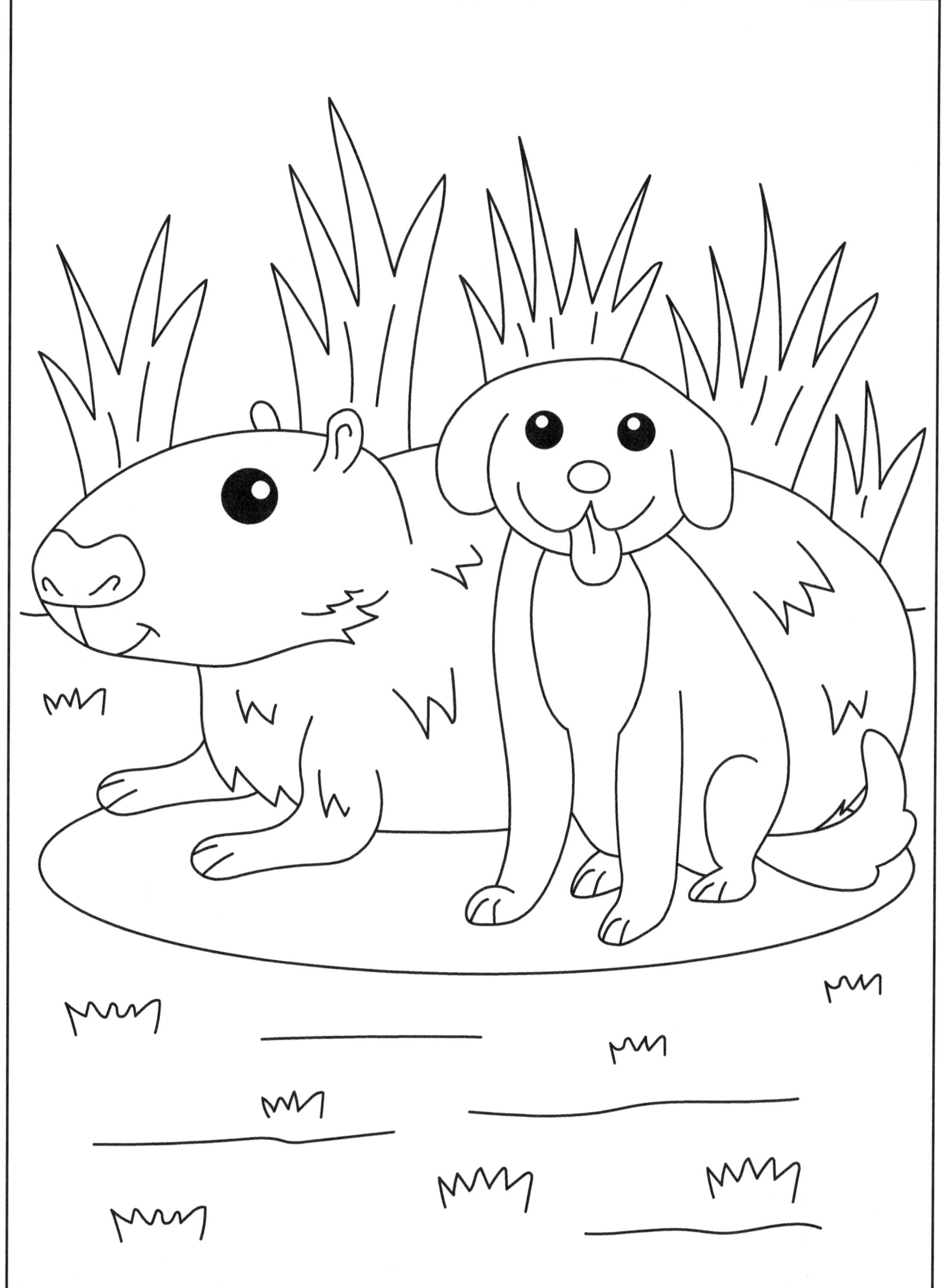

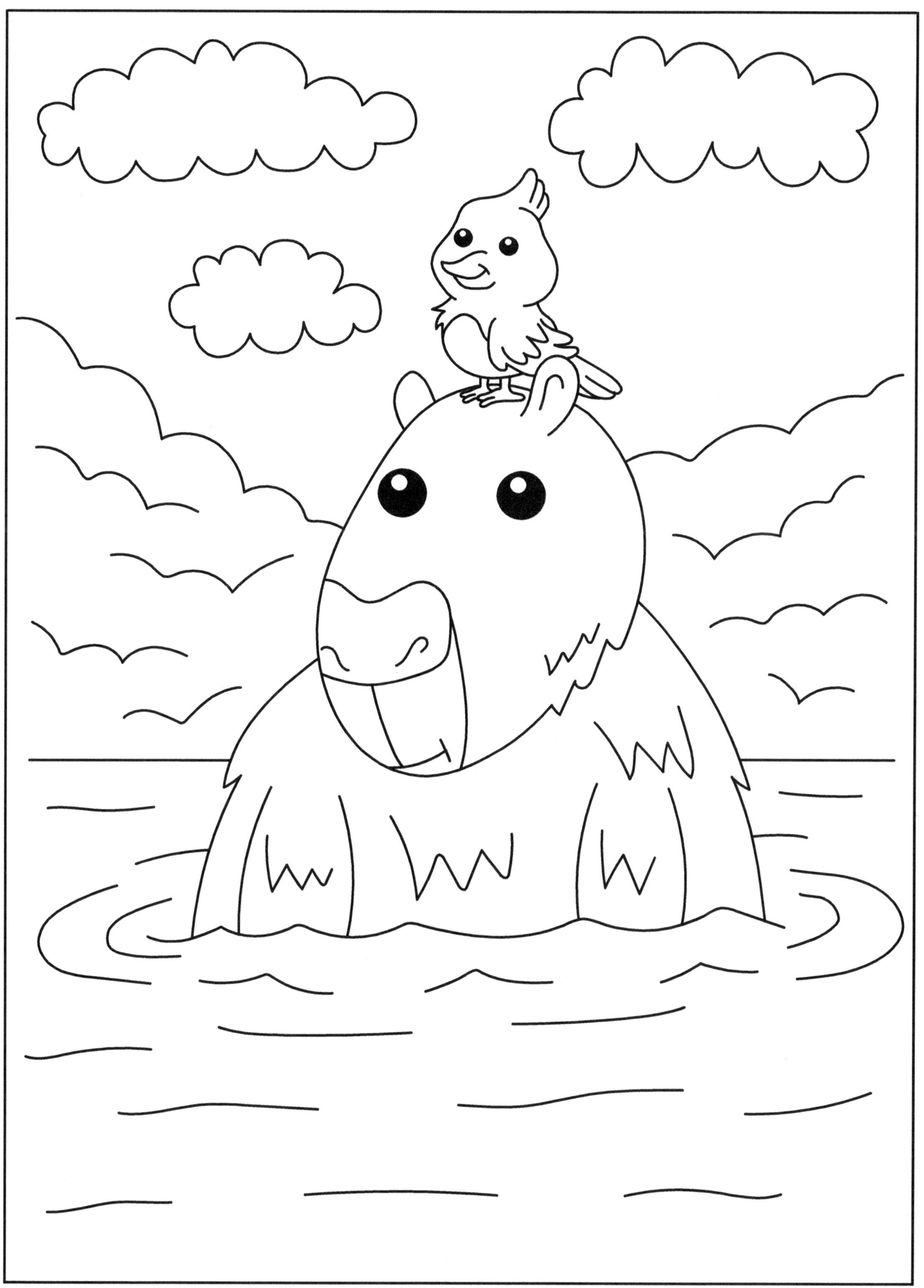

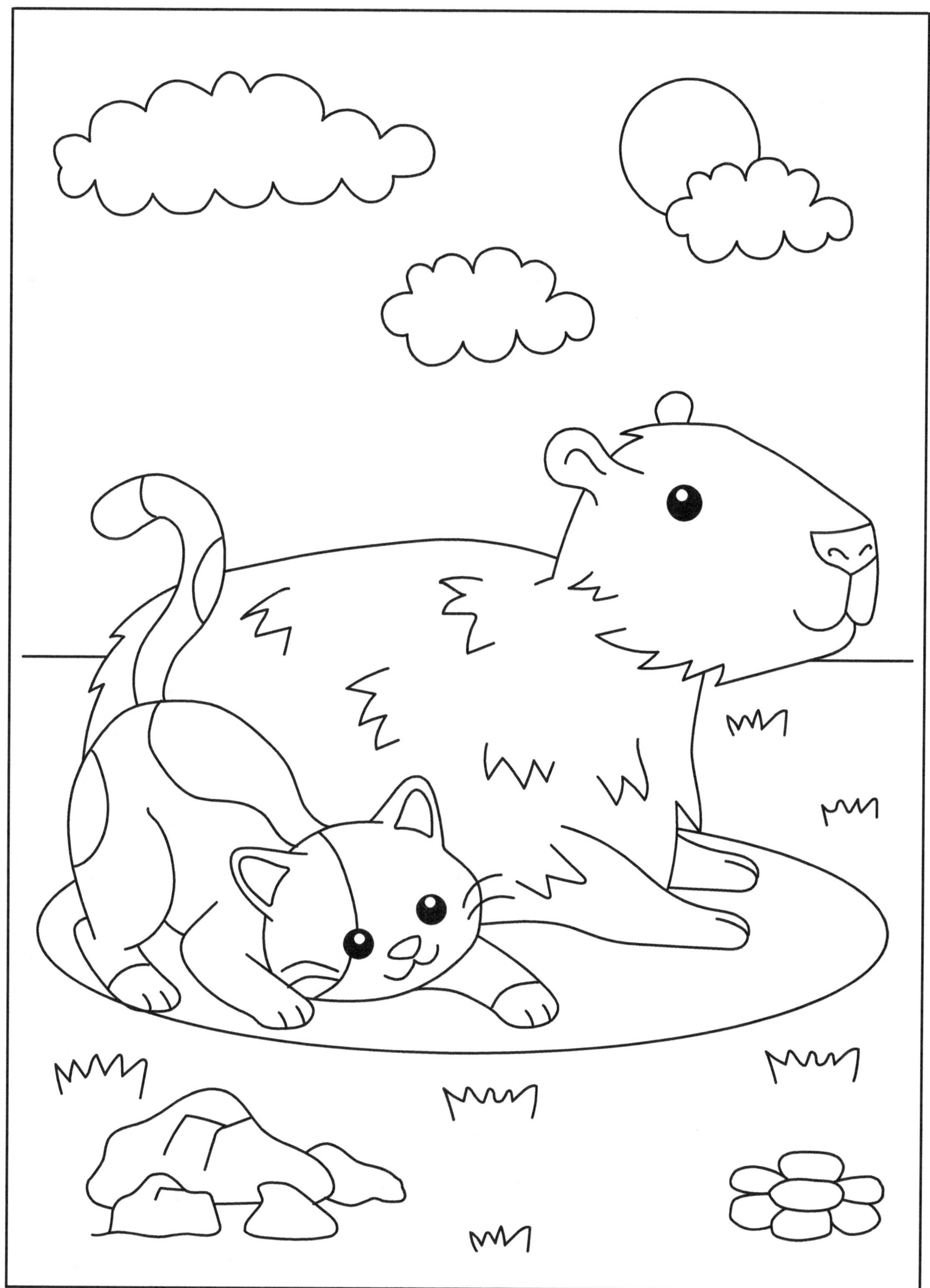

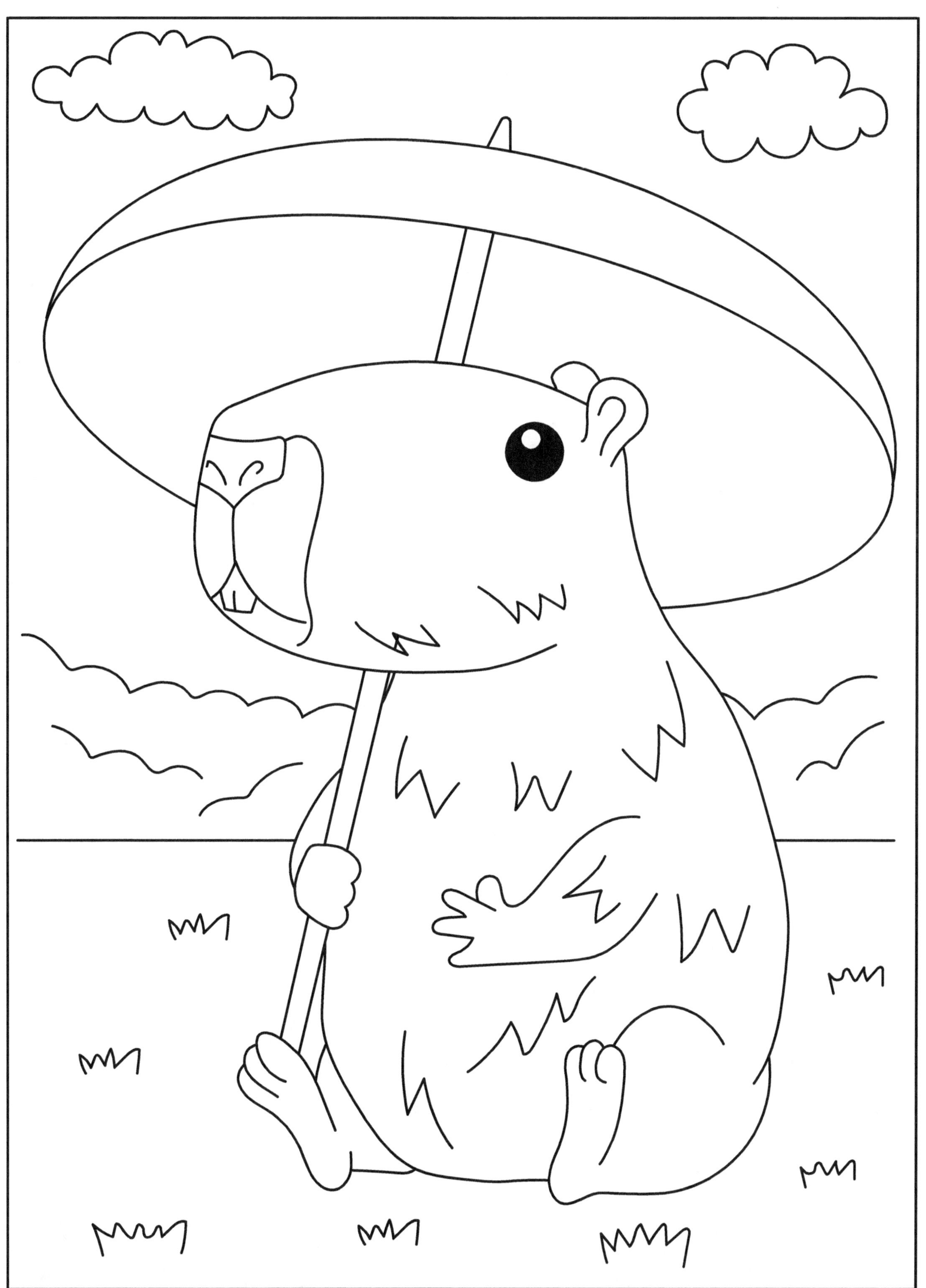

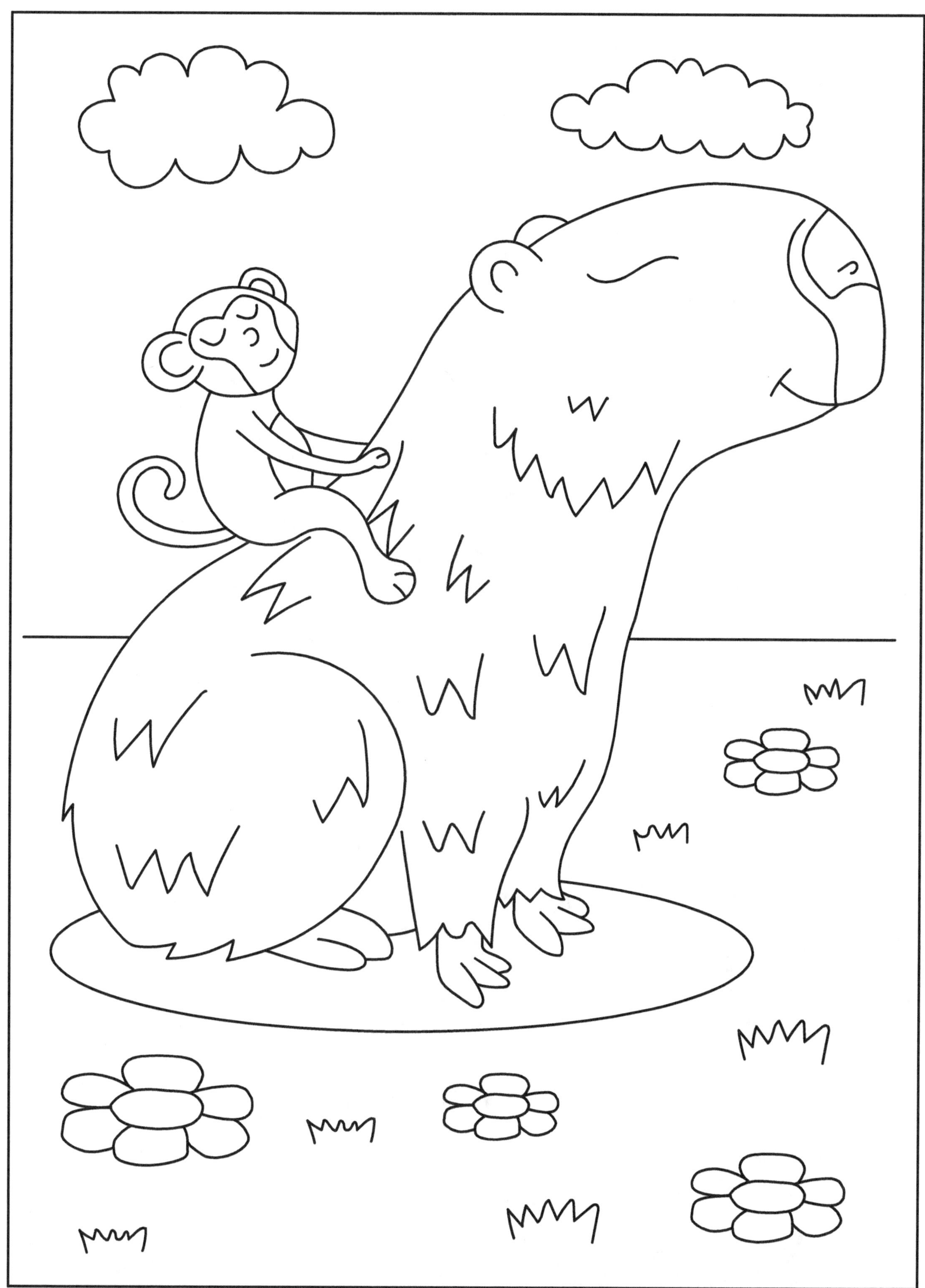

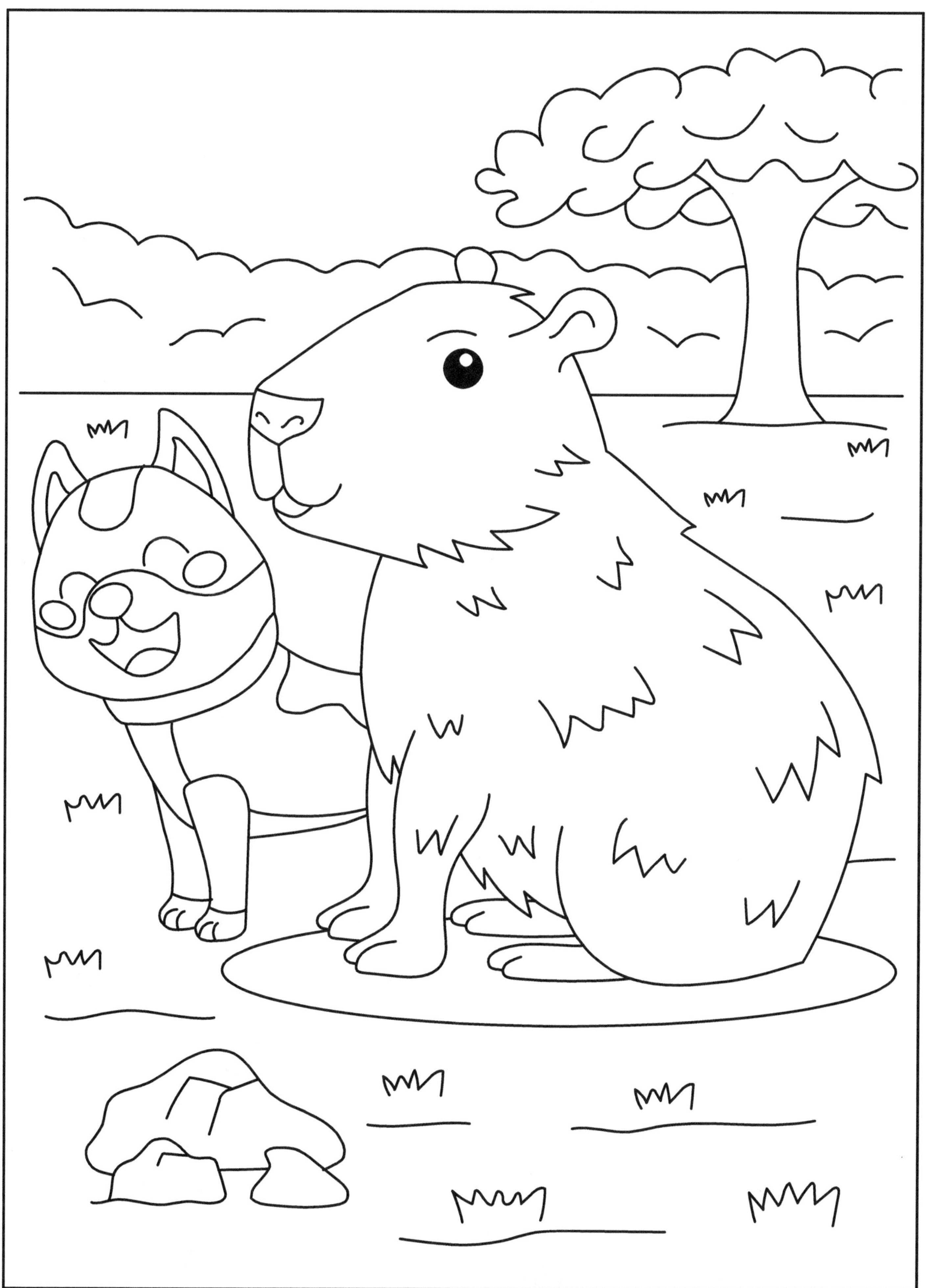